BRIGHT NOTES

OUT OF AFRICA
BY
ISAK DINESEN

Intelligent Education

Nashville, Tennessee

BRIGHT NOTES: Out of Africa
www.BrightNotes.com

No part of this publication may be used or reproduced in any manner whatsoever without written permission, except in the case of brief quotations in critical articles and reviews. For permissions, contact Influence Publishers http://www.influencepublishers.com.

ISBN: 978-1-645422-34-1 (Paperback)
ISBN: 978-1-645422-35-8 (eBook)

Published in accordance with the U.S. Copyright Office Orphan Works and Mass Digitization report of the register of copyrights, June 2015.

Originally published by Monarch Press.
Elizabeth Pardo, 1988
2019 Edition published by Influence Publishers.

Interior design by Lapiz Digital Services. Cover Design by Thinkpen Designs.

Printed in the United States of America.

Library of Congress Cataloging-in-Publication Data forthcoming.
Names: Intelligent Education
Title: BRIGHT NOTES: Out of Africa
Subject: STU004000 STUDY AIDS / Book Notes

CONTENTS

1)	Introduction to Isak Dinesen	1
2)	Dinesen's Narrative Techniques	18
3)	Textual Analysis	
	Part I: Kamante and Lulu	25
	Part II: A Shooting Accident on the Farm	40
	Part III: Visitors to the Farm	48
	Part IV: From an Immigrant's Notebook	77
	Part V: Farewell to the Farm	93
4)	Character Analyses	109
5)	Questions for Review	129
6)	Bibliography	138

INTRODUCTION TO ISAK DINESEN

DINESEN'S LIFE AND WORKS

Karen Christentze Dinesen, born April 17, 1885, was the second daughter of Ingeborg Westenholz and Wilhelm Dinesen, who was related to the greatest nobleman in the Kingdom of Denmark. According to the biographer Judith Thurman, Karen's mother and father were an "antithetical" couple, that is, they were exact opposites. The Westenholz men were traders and self-made millionaires, while the women were passionate feminists, non-conformists, and Unitarian converts. The Dinesen men tended to be virile and opinionated, and the women elegant and pretty. Though Karen Dinesen did not like her mother's family, she inherited many of their qualities and these dictated her later life. The idea that "Life seemed immoral without some calling" was a Unitarian ideal that all the Dinesen children aspired to. Karen's brother Thomas, like his father, sought fulfillment in battle and later was a writer. All three Dinesen girls showed creative and artistic talent, and Karen showed talent in both drawing and writing. She collected plots for stories, jotting down fragments and polishing them in her notebook.

Karen, also known as Tanne, a nickname she disliked but was called by her family, was the most ambitious of the siblings. At seventeen, Karen started attending drawing classes regularly in Copenhagen and later attended the Academy of Arts in Scotland, with the idea of becoming a painter.

At twenty - two, she made her debut as an author under the pseudonym "Osceola." "The Hermits" appeared in August 1907 in Tilskueren, Denmark's most distinguished literary journal. After her "The de Cats Family" appeared in the January 1909 issue of *Tilskueren*, she lost her impulse to write till later in life. This Osceola writing period reflected her religious crisis and struggles with virtue and sin, God and the Devil, and Christianity and paganism, according to some critics. Karen called her work of this period the "mystic melancholy of adolescence."

PSEUDONYM

According to biographer Judith Thurman, the pseudonym Osceola had a private meaning for Karen, and possibly was a private joke, since it was the name of her father's German shepherd that accompanied father and daughter on their walks. Wilhelm Dinesen saw and admired the American Indian Osceola as a literary figure of noble "natural man" making a last stand against extinction. Osceola (1804–38) was a leader and hero of Seminoles, born to an English father and a Creek mother. He fought against the American Government's pressure to sign a treaty that would force Indians out of Florida and into Arkansas.

FATHER'S INFLUENCE

Wilhelm was an officer first in the Danish Army and then in the French. When not at war or hunting, or in love, he was participating in Parliament as an independent with sympathies for the Liberals. Elected in 1892, the year his son Thomas was born, he wrote letters to newspapers and political pamphlets to gain support for national defense. He led Karen out of the domestic limbo and limited world of woman into the "wild." Instilling in her his great love of nature and teaching her to become observant, he guaranteed that her writing would appeal to the senses. In helping her exercise her senses he was sharing the ways of the hunter, which she regarded as a second literacy. Wilhelm stood in her mind for the sensual, uninhibited aspects of a man's life, in contrast to the women in Karen's world, with their ethical perils and self - denial. Wilhelm felt a deep affinity with the Indians, with their code of honor, their elegance, bravery, and knowledge of animals and of the wild. He romanticized their wisdom and believed they were more civilized than Europeans. This acknowledgment of the otherness, of the Native and his romanticized visions of civilization and nature, left their permanent mark on Karen's life.

FIRST PERSONAL TRAGEDY

Karen's first great grief was her father's suicide when she was ten. Wilhelm killed himself by hanging, a dishonorable death, since it was the method used by the army to execute its deserters. This conscious choice of death may have been his final gesture of betrayal of wife, family, and political loyalties. Having contracted syphilis he was doomed to live a wretched life; he may not have been able to endure it, being an outdoor man and soldier. According to Thurman, Karen at fifteen became "obsessed by the idea that her father lived on in her." She romanticizes her father in "The Hermits" and he appears as a melancholy figure in "Copenhagen."

GENESIS OF OUT OF AFRICA

The influence of Wilhelm cannot be said to be the only influence in Karen's later writings but it had major impact. Ideas from Wilhelm's Letters from the Hunt, his **themes** of survival and of the price of one's existence appear in her works. According to her biographer, since her youth Karen tried to "realize" an idea and anticipate her life's destiny by making an old story come true. The story she had planned to act out in her life was actually meant to be the "requiem" of her father's story. The ideas of serenity in the wilderness, the courage and simplicity of primal peoples, and nature as a moral force are all lessons learned from her father that are incorporated in *Out of Africa*.

FORESHADOWING OF SECOND TRAGEDY

When her love for her second cousin, Baron Hans Blixen - Finecke, was not acknowledged or returned, she married his twin brother, Baron Bror Blixen - Finecke of Nasbyholm. It was a marriage of convenience. Her story "The Old Chevalier" evokes the experience of first love and explores the problems of unrequited love.

Bror, known for his stamina, is believed to have been a model for Hemingway's great white hunter, Robert Wilson, in "The Short Happy Life of Francis Macomber." Though Bror had the erotic impertinence of her father, he lacked finesse, intelligence and integrity. Their marriage was a mutual exploitation with real affection on both sides. Bror had a title and connections with the highest nobility, including the Swedish royal family. But more importantly, it was the Westenholz fortune that underwrote the farm they bought in Kenya. "The Dreaming Child" in Dinesen's *Winter Tales* includes her explanation of the marriage of convenience as practiced by Copenhagen women.

ON TO AFRICA

Robert Langbaum, one of Isak Dinesen's best critics, describes how she "rediscovered in Africa the validity of all the romantic myths which locate the spirit in the elemental - in nature, in the life of primitive people, in instinct and passion, and in aristocratic, feudal and tribal society which have their roots in nature."

When she married Baron Bror in 1913 and went to Africa, she joined the early white settlers in the newly established British colony, Kenya, in East Africa, and for the next seventeen years unsuccessfully attempted to make a coffee plantation profitable.

LIFE TRAGEDY TWO

Karen chose the men in her life who were like her father: unavailable and unreliable. Bror proved unfit to be a farm manager because of his unreliability over money. He also showed no discretion about his affairs with a friend's wife or with African women, mostly the Masai women who had a high rate of venereal diseases.

Karen contracted syphilis, like her father, and came to believe her father's destiny had been repeated in her own destiny. As a result of the syphilis she became sterile. When she finally confessed to her mother in a letter that she and Bror had separated, she begged her mother not to share the news with the family. In an Autumn 1921 letter she expressed the trauma of her father's death as the greatest misfortune. She felt he had deserted her. Nevertheless, "Father understood me as I was, ... loved me for myself."

OTHER INFLUENCES

References to Georg Brandes, Hume, Nietzche, classical mythology, Shelley, Shakespeare, and the Bible are found in most of her works. Karen credits Georg Brandes, the great Scandinavian critic thought to be a corruptor of youth, with revealing literature to her. Karen's attraction to the greatest critic of the age was enhanced by the fact that he knew her father well. Romantic traditions in her tales were influenced by Brandes' intellectual history of Romanticism. It was Brandes who introduced her to the relatively unknown Nietzsche in his lectures "On Aristocratic Radicalism." Brandes also helped Karen publish the marionette play *The Revenge of Truth*.

REPUTATION AS A STORYTELLER

Most of Dinesen's tales are embroiled in the spirit of storytelling; a basic **theme** in all her tales is the storyteller's defense of the art of the story. She spoke of herself as Scheherazade, whose life depended on keeping the thread of the tales going through *The Thousand and One Nights* so that the Sultan never lost interest. She holds the readers' interest by involving them in the story.

One writer saw Dinesen "perform" one of her tales. She had the "trance-like stare of the soothsayer living wholly in another space and time." Her study of painting and art is revealed in her writing when she paints landscapes with words, as in *Out of*

Africa and *Shadows on the Grass*. Her admiration of great painters is evident in her tale "The Deluge of Nordency." Dinesen saw herself as clearly belonging to the oral tradition of literature. She believed her tales have "an almost physical or instinctual source, like the dance," according to her biographer.

PSEUDONYMS

For her major works Karen Blixen adopted the pseudonym "Isak Dinesen." This name indicates her rediscovering herself by redefining herself. Isak, a Hebrew masculine name meaning "one who laughs," emphasizes the masculine side of her nature. Dinesen, her father's name, indicates her desire to stay connected to her father. She decided to use this pseudonym, at the age of 48, with the completion of Seven Gothic Tales, in the hope of avoiding excessive negative attention. The use of a pseudonym is a way of erasing the author's social identity.

DINESEN'S AFRICA

Dinesen left Denmark to expose herself to a life unprotected by society, to "find herself," as Brandes would advise, to protect wild animals, wilder outcasts, deserters from Europe, the adventurers turned guides and Safari Hunter, all in memory of her father. Her Africa is a different Africa from Elspeth Huxley's accounts of her early years in Kenya (as in *The Flame Trees of Thika* and *The Mottled Lizard*; *White Man's Country* is her history of the colony). *Out of Africa* is told as a visionary flight of fancy in which everything seems more than it is.

Out of Africa, written five years after Dinesen left Africa for good, deals with a period already set back in the past.

The distancing of time and place better enabled her to reflect about her African experience. Dinesen altered and rearranged the actual facts of her years in Africa to fit the purpose of the storyteller. She describes picturesque moments without chronology or any hint of how much time has elapsed. No details of her life prior to Kenya are included; intimate self revelations are left out so as not to distract the reader. Omissions about her life also concealed agonizing defeats in her personal life. In another book, *Letters from Africa*, she reveals her truly personal feelings about her experiences in Africa. In Thomas Dinesen's *My Sister, Isak* we find still other facts that she had not revealed in *Out of Africa*.

LOSS - PERSONAL TRAGEDY THREE

When Dinesen realized that leaving Africa was inevitable, she perceived parting with Africa as "Armageddon." The loss of the farm and the death of her lover, Denys Finch Hatton, whom she considered a true aristocrat, were the two events that determined her own destiny and future as a writer.

Isak Dinesen - the Baroness Karen Dinesen Blixen - died in 1962, aged 77, from emaciation after long suffering from syphilis.

DINESEN'S THEMES

THEMES: EXPLICIT AND IMPLICIT

During and after an experience with good fiction, we naturally reflect on its subject, central ideas, thesis, message, moral, its overall meaning. And pulling together all the conclusions we can derive from a story, we find it convenient to designate them with a catchall word: themes. We sometimes refer to one aspect of a **theme**, a subtheme, as a motif. We may consider our inferences to be valid if our formulations of the **themes** and motifs prove to be interrelated and overlapping.

Sometimes an author states his **themes** explicitly, outright, either in his own authorial voice (e.g., Dinesen's **theme** of civilization and nature) or more subtly, through his characters' own statements of their beliefs and conclusions. Thus, many of Dinesen's **themes** can be found in dialogue involving the natives and Dinesen, and aristocrats and Dinesen. We know that Dinesen intends their intellectual observations to be thematic because she makes them all sympathetic characters. We know the author does not intend us to take our philosophy of life from Baron Bror because she makes him unattractive: his ideas seem to be inherent in his unpleasant personality.

At other times the author will use the subtle, artistic means of expressing themes. She allows us to derive her meaning from the conduct and fate of her characters, from the outcome of their actions. Thus, we learn about Dinesen's view of organized religion from the Missions' behavior and the author's attitude toward the natives from the shooting incident. Such themes are expressed implicitly.

Dinesen seems to offer these ideas, explicit or implicit, as her main **themes** in *Out of Africa*:

ARISTOCRACY AND NOBILITY

The characters and descriptive landscapes reflect Dinesen's idea of aristocracy. The idea of "noblesse oblige" (i.e., "rank has its obligations"), is embodied by the fearless Africans, Dinesen's favorite English aristocrats - Berkeley Cole and Denys Finch - Hatton - as well as by her African servants, Farah and Kamante, and the wild animals. Dinesen invests in the natives many heroic and aristocratic character traits. The aristocratic attribute she gives to the "noble savage," Kinanjui, is that of a great chief with a fortitude of soul like "an old warrior."

The Masai, a warrior tribe, typify the qualities in life she admires: pride, fearlessness, nobility. She considers them the true aristocrats of spirit. A young Masai warrior, Kabero, is described as a "statue" to be seen and admired. Using analogical language to describe her picturesque Africa, her intention is to convey a feeling of nobility, greatness, and pride. The mountain of Ngong is described as being "crowned with noble peaks" with a view of "unequaled nobility."

Dinesen links the natural aristocracy of Africa with traditional European aristocracy. She makes the connection of the primitive and aristocratic virtues in her work as Hemingway does in his African tales.

HEROIC IDEAL

The grandeur of the descriptions in Dinesen's work furnishes the background for the heroic nature of life she believes in. In her turning away from a domesticated world to the undomesticated Africa, she attempts to live up to the heroic ideal. The artist who becomes a proud, noble figure, dedicated to a lonely existence, with a heroic attitude amidst isolation, reflects Lord Byron's attitude of self - assertion. Dinesen's struggle to "become herself" and support her "new nobility" is disclosed in the epigraph taken from Nietzsche's Thus Spake Zarathustra:

"Equitare, Arcum tendere, Veritatem dicere," that is, "to ride, to shoot with a bow, to tell the truth." A class of people who have learned to know life through actions and have a use for history are the noble class, according to Nietzsche. The African's heroic dimensions lie in their philosophy of life, their attitude toward pain and death, which echoes Yeats' heroic idea, "a cold eye on life, on death." Dinesen's heroic perspectives are evident in her characterization of African tribes. The fury, pride, and stubborn independence of the Somali tribe are experienced through her daily dealings with them, and through her mention of the Masai warrior tribes' memories of battles and heroic deeds. Kamante is portrayed as an example of heroic defiance and is described by Dinesen in terms of a quote from Shelley's *Prometheus Unbound*: "Pain is my element as hate is thine." Kamante, despite the fact that his legs were covered with deep running sores, faced his pain and appeared heroic to Dinesen. Even the wild animals in the story are described as noble, gracious, heroic figures.

CIVILIZATION LOST AND THE FALL

Dinesen's admiration of the Natives was for their knowledge of nature and their natural way of doing things. Unlike Europeans, who had lost their knowledge of nature, the Natives maintained an umbilical cord with nature and lived within "their own element," according to Dinesen. She perceives the Natives as not distinguishing between themselves and the rest of nature; they are still innocent, or the "unfallen" in the African Eden, which is an authentic parallel to Milton's Eden in *Paradise Lost*. Unlike Hemingway, who sees Africa as the state of nature we lost, Dinesen sees Africa as a kind of civilization we have lost. Dinesen perceives modern life as cut off from a traditional civilization that had its roots in nature. Dinesen's desire to seek harmony with nature is expressed as a profound sense of fulfillment:

"Here I am, where I ought to be." Dinesen's words and ideas about nature support the romantic myth of the alienated artists of the nineteenth century who saw nature and civilization as being in harmony with one another. The right kind of civilization would be a means to recover the natural virtues lost in the fall.

THE FALL

Each part of the story can be seen as an example of idyllic life, followed by the fall. The fall in this story is the development of the new European order or industrialization, a taking over (destroying of nature's innocence). The final fall is caused by adverse forces of nature and historical change that causes Dinesen to lose her African Eden and end her personal "Golden Age."

GOD

Fate, Destiny, and Pride are all part of Dinesen's perception of God. The Natives, unlike the Europeans, do not attempt "to insure themselves against the assaults of fate." Dinesen's admiration of this quality is in agreement with Nietzsche's belief that "fate should be courageously embraced," a lesson taken from the Book of Job. Natives adjust to the unforeseen and are accustomed to the unexpected. They are on "friendly terms with destiny," according to Dinesen.

NATIVES' IDEA OF GOD

Imagination ranks high among the qualities sought in a master, doctor, or god by the Natives, according to Dinesen. So it is not surprising to discover that Haroun - al - Raschid, the Caliph of Baghdad, is considered an ideal ruler by Natives since he is unpredictable. Dinesen states, "When the Africans speak of the personality of God, they speak of Arabian Nights or the last chapter of the Book of Job."

THE FATE OF JOB

The God of the Book of Job is the all - powerful God whole imagination transcends human comprehension and against whom it is foolish to rebel. The pagan Africans understand that the nature of experience is neither good nor evil, neither sacred nor profane. Understanding this **irony** makes them seem worldlier than their Christian masters, since the Natives know that what matters is the recognition that God's power and imagination transcend all understanding. The Natives preserved the knowledge, Dinesen believes, lost to most Europeans, that God and the Devil are one, "the majesty coeternal." Dinesen's belief in God is revealed by Emmanuelson's answer. When she asked if he believed in God, he replied that God was the only thing he did believe in. (see p. 28)

Other references to the Book of Job are found in the latter part of the novel and relate to tragic loss. Dinesen describes the Natives' religion and their dependency on God when faced with drought, fever, coffee disease, and the loss of the farm. Drought was perceived as punishment from the Great Power. Afflictions suffered were, like the afflictions of Job, seemingly distributed by malicious powers, which Dinesen believed laughed at her at the end. Dinesen states she felt like the man in her stork parable or a marionette.

Dinesen's little story of the chameleon and the cock suggests God's capacity to be malicious, but also served as a sign. Dinesen was feeling like Shakespeare's Lear when all events had lost their **rhyme** or reason. A brave gray chameleon stuck out his tongue to mock his enemy, a big white cock. This story can be regarded as Dinesen's realization that malicious powers could only be defied proudly, with laughter and above all courage, like the type the Natives had.

DESTINY

Two paragraphs in Dinesen's Part IV ("From an Immigrant's Notebook") reflect her perceptions of man's choices and his destiny. These paragraphs are seen by Hannah Arendt as an expression of an "artistic creed": loyalty to the story, to the ideas of the author, to a greater imagination.

Pride, as Dinesen sees it, is understanding the work of God as being the "right arrangement." "Humility is understanding that within this arrangement God has no favorites." The idea that everyone has the choice to play his role in life or not, in order to fulfill his own destiny, is a **theme** presented in this book as well as in her other works. Active cooperation with God, and realizing God's intentions, are what's necessary to fulfill one's destiny.

The parable of the stork supports Dinesen's idea on destiny. The moral lesson of the parable was that a man that kept his faith and cause and the design of life was rewarded with seeing a stork. He could be considered a good marionette, since he had performed his expected role and carried out God's design. In her expressed idea of pride, it is clear that people have the doubtful privilege of being able to struggle against destiny, or so against the grand design, successfully, since man's happiness lies "in his fulfillment of his fate." Dinesen defines God as "a guarding principle" in the universe. He creates, for each individual, choice and the need to decide exactly what their guiding principle consists of and how to follow it in their own lives. This **theme** is evident too in Dinesen's The Revenge of Truth and Winter's Tale.

CHRISTIAN DOCTRINE

The marionette symbol is referred to again, when Dinesen questions the second article of faith of the Christian Church. Dinesen asks: "What ups and downs are as terrible as those of the man in the story?" Christ is seen as different from ordinary marionettes in his role and rewards. Christ can be seen as a mythical figure, since he too had to realize his destiny.

Dinesen, through her description of the locations of the missions, indicates her disapproval or distrust of their actual "mission." The Church of Scotland's mission was 500 feet higher than the farm, but not any closer to God. This mission gave Dinesen an impression of blindness, as if it could see nothing itself, when she implies that their intentions to change the Natives were not genuine, not for salvation; their concern was for getting the Natives to wear European clothes. The French Roman Catholic Mission, which was 500 feet lower, was the Church she was able most to relate to and was most friendly with.

CHRIST AND THE NATIVES

Dinesen uses the symbol of the fish when she refers to the natives' lack of fear. The fish is an ancient fertility symbol that in Christianity represents Christ. The Natives, like Christ, also accepted suffering as part of life. (Nietzsche said life is good because of suffering, not in spite of it.) Kamante, the Kikuyu, comes back from the Church of Scotland Mission cured of his sores but also "scarred." He comes back a Christian, on Easter Sunday, like Christ, after much suffering. He comes to live with Dinesen with the understanding that he is like her, and attaches his fate to hers.

Dinesen's disapproval of the missions' intentions may be related to Nietzsche's idea that Christianity beckons man's thoughts away from this world, and does not teach men how to live, but how to die. Missions, as seen by Dinesen, were really stifling human freedom. This is a belief of most Romantics, along with their concern with the nature of transcendent reality.

DIVINE PERSONA

Dinesen is perceived by the Natives as God, master, counselor, doctor, and judge. Her story - telling has godlike powers. From the beginning of her story, she is the "air" in the hills, high above it all, next to God. The Natives invested what they knew of God in her, in other matters as well when they needed a judge. Her biographer has implied Dinesen is the "redeemer" who suffers an exemplary "death" so that she could hold out the promise of "spiritual freedom," and like Christ, give up her life for the people. Her story transforms human purpose into divine purpose.

FEUDALISM

Dinesen ruled like an eighteenth-century feudal lord over her six - thousands - acre coffee plantation, with squatters holding a few acres in return for a few days of work on the plantation. In her beautiful, well organized, formal world, there are references to the landscape, animals, and people as fitting a pattern or a tapestry. Dinesen also writes about the feudal society in relation to the rhythms of Africa, as she describes movement, stillness of people, and wild animals. Dinesen took up her position in an aristocratic hierarchy based on semi - feudal conditions. As landowner, she felt responsible for the people, and carried out her duties with pride. Romantic mythology is evident as Dinesen attempts to reconstruct the organic life of a European past - the Middle Ages.

NATURE

Africa has the sense of the timeless life of Nature where landscape, animals, and events merge. Some descriptions of Africa compare to elements of a dream, as in the Arabian Nights, where things of a good dream happen. Dinesen's view from her house indicates that the line between nature and civilization is passable. The references to the animals she can see from her home indicate this passability. Through her description of animals and landscape, Dinesen idealizes civilization's counterpart in the forest and animal kingdom. According to Dinesen, in order to achieve a higher form of civilization, an understanding of the wild is necessary.

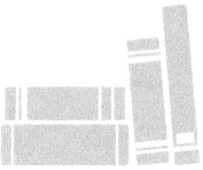

OUT OF AFRICA

DINESEN'S NARRATIVE TECHNIQUES

GENRE

Dinesen's *Out of Africa* is an artistic account of her 17-year (1914–1931) experience while running a farm in Kenya, British East Africa. It includes stories and portraits of her relationships with many Europeans, Asians, and Africans, some of them important historically, most of them important to her personally; impressions of the Natives at large; accounts of her service in the African Theatre of World War I as an "irregular"; and splendid descriptions of the African landscape and of her own psychological states and philosophical musings and the situations that helped create them. Because of its implicit demonstration of the equality of women it can also be considered a feminist document as well as an historical-social and literary document.

Dinesen's *Out of Africa* has been variously classified as an autobiographical narrative, a memoir, and a prose pastoral. It is difficult to classify this book as belonging neatly to any one literary genre.

AUTOBIOGRAPHICAL NARRATIVE

That the work is an autobiographical narrative is true with certain qualifications. It is not a complete autobiographical account of Dinesen's life or even of those 17 years. She omits, for example, almost all details about her marriage (which was what brought her to Africa in the first place), about her divorce, about the romantic side of her friendship with Denys Finch - Hatton, and about some important visitors like her brother and mother. She also changes some autobiographical details, e.g., she alters the story of a lion hunt to give herself credit for one lion actually shot by Finch - Hatton. This then is autobiographical narrative enhanced for artistic purposes: essentially true but not always literally true, and on occasion, actually fictitious.

A MEMOIR

Dinesen's book is closer to a memoir, if we describe the memoir as a record of events written by a person with intimate knowledge of them and based on personal observation and experience. The memoirist, unlike the autobiographer, is not expected to give a complete account but rather one that emphasizes certain aspects of his or her experience that would be of public interest. The last phrase could be crucial here. Usually the word memoir connotes writing by or about someone already well known, e.g., a work written about a President or a diplomat by his personal secretary. But personal accounts like Dinesen's also qualify if they throw light on some historical situation, as Dinesen's does on the colonization of Africa and on the role of women, white and black, during the period 1914–1931.

PROSE PASTORAL

Dinesen's *Out of Africa* has also been classified as a prose pastoral. The pastoral is one of the oldest literary genres. As conceived by Theocritus (c. 308-c. 240 B.C.E.) in his Idylls, the pastoral poem presents a very idealized picture of the simple lives and loves of shepherds. Virgil (70–19 B.C.E.) added to the **genre** a new level of meaning with his social commentary. During the Renaissance, pastoral included not only poetic works about rural life (e.g., Edmund Spenser's *The Shepherd's Calendar*) but also prose (fictional) pastorals (e.g., Sir Phillip Sidney's *Arcadia*), and pastoral drama (e.g., John Fletcher's *The Faithful Shepherdess*). Twentieth - century poets who have worked in the pastoral tradition, with strong Virgilian **didactic** intent, include Robert Frost and Allen Ginsberg.

The basic idea of the pastoral is that it idealizes, or expresses nostalgia for, the rural life, and/or that it uses rural settings to comment on urban life or on civilization generally.

Dinesen's *Out of Africa* qualifies as a pastoral on both counts, and adds to the **genre** of poetic, dramatic, and fictional prose pastorals a sterling example of the nonfictional prose pastoral.

OVERALL STRUCTURE

Dinesen does not follow a strictly chronological order in her account of life in and around her farm. Rather she arranges her reminiscences into five parts that both (1) gradually broaden the scope of her narrative and (2) typify the long rise and the sudden fall of her fortunes.

Thus her Part I, "Kamante and Lulu," consists of four chapters that focus on the farm, its mistress, her Native cook, and their favorite pet, a wild animal temporarily domesticated.

Dinesen broadens the scope in Part II, "A Shooting Accident on the Farm," to include the peoples and landscape of a much larger region, mainly as she becomes involved with them because of a bloody accident that occurs in a farm kitchen.

She devotes Part III to the "Visitors to the Farm," starting from casual and social acquaintances and building up to her more friendly and passionate relationships, rising to the peak of her happiness as symbolized and typified in her airplane flights with Finch - Hatton.

Part IV, "From an Immigrant's Notebook," she reserves for thirty - two miscellaneous sketches that both keep us on a plateau of suspense, broaden our experience of her "rise," and foreshadow her "fall."

She combines in Part V, "Farewell to the Farm," several tragic events that led to her loss of the farm and her psychological near - collapse. (Again, she selects and rejects, not detailing, for example, the way her ex - husband's mis - management had foredoomed their project.)

INTERNAL STRUCTURES

Within its place in the overall structure, Dinesen organizes each chapter either logically or chronologically. Thus in each introduction she either states the topic of that chapter or section and relates it to other chapters, or she starts a slow suspenseful buildup to the main situation. We shall note later on the sections that are also dramatic in structure.

Dinesen in this book is a great believer in the topic sentence, that is, a sentence, usually at the beginning of a paragraph, that sums up what the paragraph is all about. The overwhelming majority of her paragraphs in Parts I, II, III, and V start with topic sentences. Some topic sentences are so important she makes them stand alone; in this case they may state the topic or direction of several paragraphs to come.

STYLE AND TONE

Within her clearly outlined structures, Dinesen develops her material in a seemingly casual, almost at times free - associational manner. But she is always economical with words. Her sentences are always varied in length and in structure, establishing a rhythm suitable to the subject. Her tone varies from that of the nonfiction writer judiciously explaining the difference between Kikuyu and Anglo - Saxon legal procedures, to that of the enthusiastic lover of fauna and flora, to that of the satirist. In one chapter, "The Shooting Accident," she goes suddenly from her idyllic, pastoral tone to her bloody - realistic tone.

STYLE: METAPHOR

Dinesen writes poetic prose of the highest order. She is a master of both **metaphor** and **simile**. Such comparisons state a similarity between dissimilars in such a way that we are surprised, shocked into seeing a new relationship. When a writer like Dinesen produces a steady stream of poetic comparisons, she is also adding to the suspense because the reader is eager to find the next such metaphoric excitement. Thus Dinesen delights us by viewing grey fungus hanging from trees as "long drooping beards" ("A Gazelle"), gazelles coming to a green place to graze as "toy animals stood upon a billiard table" ("Riding in the Reserve"), and the African night as similar to the nave of a great cathedral ("The Shooting Accident"). She even ventures a Homeric simile ("Wanyangerri"). All these devices will be discussed in greater detail in our "Textual Analysis."

STYLE: ALLUSIONS

A voracious reader all her life, who read poetry aloud with her friends and relatives, Dinesen cinches many of her points by making **allusions** to literature, mythology, and history. Some of the authors and works she resorts to are *The Arabian Nights*, the Bible (Genesis, Job, Esther, etc.), Samuel Taylor Coleridge, Percy Shelley, Lord Byron, Heinrich Heine, Giovanni Boccaccio, Sappho, and William Shakespeare. She does not always identify the work she alludes to. In this Bright Note we shall identify each **allusion**, and explain its relevance, in our "Textual Analysis."

STYLE: CONTRASTS

We always understand better the point Dinesen is making - or just see her characters better - because she revels in comparisons, especially in contrasts. Thus she notes in detail the differences between certain city girls and certain country girls, she compares the Kikuyu tribe with the Masai, she contrasts the poor plaintiff with the rich defendant, and she is always eager to explore differences between men and women.

SENSUOUS DETAILS

Dinesen appeals not only to our intellect but to all our senses. Each scene is rich in smell, sound, touch, and taste as well as sights. In "Old Knudsen" she makes us aware of "the piercing, fresh, rank, sour smell of the burning kiln." In "Wings," we see all color "scorched out" of the sky, we pick up the saline scent of burnt grass, and we feel the morning air like deep - sea currents.

We shall identify and discuss, in greater detail, Dinesen's style and tone, her use of analogical language, allusions, contrasts, and sense appeal, and her other literary devices, in our "Chapter - by -Chapter Textual Analysis."

OUT OF AFRICA

TEXTUAL ANALYSIS

PART I: KAMANTE AND LULU

THE NGONG FARM

Title

Dinesen chooses as her first chapter title an exotic phrase guaranteed to arouse our curiosity: a farm named Ngong.

Style

Sensuous details are established through the use of analogical language. Comparative descriptions appeal to the reader's five senses. The reader is invited to partake of the African experience. Part of Dinesen's design is to compel the reader's imagination to participate in the storyteller's creation. The colors and their descriptions appeal to our sense of sight as the storyteller paints the landscape with language. The invitation to smell the grass "spiced with thyme" and to use other senses adds to the exotic atmosphere of paradise.

Implicit comparisons (metaphors) and explicit comparisons (similes) are used to describe people and animals. Animals are seen as bits of landscape, as the Rhino that is described as a big angular stone. Elephants pacing are personified as having human concerns. The Natives are seen as variants of the wildlife, implying their natural place in Africa.

Setting

The setting is described in dream - like terms that materialize out of the African land. From the very first line of the story, a dreamlike memory of something already lost is implied by the word "had." "I had a farm... ." The way of life and world being described has disappeared or is in the process of disappearing, but is kept alive by the storyteller's belief in its existence. The air is considered the chief feature of the landscape; it is life sustaining.

Style: diction

The generous use of figurative language that creates picturesque images, coupled with the storyteller's use of rhetoric, creates an atmosphere of nobility, greatness, and pride. The mountains of Ngong are described as being "crowned with four noble peaks," with a "majestic" summit, under "proud floating" clouds.

Style: contrasts

Nairobi, though the capital of Kenya where the government is housed, seems nothing next to the Ngong Farm. The farm is described as being a thousand feet higher than Nairobi, and here height is symbolic of superiority. The description of Nairobi itself is loaded with words like "burning hot," "dusty," "motley" that create an image of uncomfortableness and "uncivilized" existence. The fact that the town is everchanging and compared to running water gives the reader a sense of its lack of integrity. The description of the town and how dysfunctional it seems is a condemnation of the new European order, while the farm is clearly a representation of the old.

Characterization: Natives and Europeans

That the Natives have their own biases and pride is shown in the explanation of tribal customs and conflicts. Nevertheless, the Natives are represented positively and described as "dignified, intelligent" people. The Somali tribe's indifference to surroundings is contrasted with the European's idea of home. Admiration for the Somalis' risk-taking and fearlessness of death or pain is contrasted with the European's constant avoidance of pain and fear of death. Natives are thought to have the preserved knowledge of God and Devil as a Unity that Europeans have lost. Europeans, says Dinesen, did not allow themselves to see the Natives as people and therefore were not sensitive to the Natives' feelings. The squatter's land is described as being more alive, in contrast to Dinesen's five thousand acres, as if it's their being part of their land that makes things grow.

"Right kind of civilization"

The formal and ideological structure Dinesen perceives Africa to be suggests to the reader what she thinks of as the right kind of civilization. Her feeling "Here I am, where I ought to be" suggests that being in harmony with nature is how a higher civilization could be achieved. The Natives' streak of malice and delight in things gone wrong is seen as revolting to Europeans. Still, Natives are seen by Dinesen as more "civilized." She admires their knowledge of nature and their place in it.

Feudalism

The idea of a feudal arrangement on the farm is introduced early as a contrast between Dinesen's world and that of the Natives. Note that squatters who live in huts called "shambas" are members of the Kikuyu tribe that holds one thousand acres compared to her five thousand. Their reverence to her as "Msabu" establishes her position as a type of feudal lord. The Hunted and the Hunter perform a necessary dance of survival, but they also must be attuned to Nature's music. The reader infers that learning the rhythm of Africa and being attuned to Nature's music is the way to achieve a higher civilization. Dinesen implies that what she has learned from the game of the country, who are in direct contact with God, has aided her in dealing with the Natives; it has set "the routine of daily life to the orchestra."

Literary allusions

The Biblical **allusion** to King Solomon's favorite horse, coupled with the wind named Monsoon, implies how God is indeed watching and gives the highlands the feeling of being blessed by God. Another possible interpretation is that the favorite horse, from a King known not only for his wisdom, but for his fabulous horse stables as well, graces Arabia and Africa with its presence.

The mythical **allusion** to Fata Morgana means that the magical quality of Africa's sparkling water evokes images of a fairy who figured in medieval legends and romance.

A NATIVE CHILD

Characterization: figurative language

Dinesen uses figurative language to suggest significant likenesses between people and animals. To create a comic effect as well as suggest some significant character traits Kamante possesses, she compares him to "a dark bat with very big spreading ears," and to "a small African Will - o' - the - wisp, with a lamp in his hand." Kamante makes Dinesen think of a gargoyle who may have sat on top of the Cathedral of Notre Dame of Paris. Dinesen also describes him as having the eyes of a dead person to illustrate how resigned, and completely closed to all surrounding life Kamante is.

Allusions

The Biblical **allusion** to the Book of Job illustrates the belief in the "infinite power of imagination" and the Natives' acceptance of destiny from an imaginative God. The literary **allusion** to *The Arabian Nights* has to do with fate and imagination. To illustrate Kamante's endurance for pain and suffering, Dinesen alludes to Shelley's lines from *Prometheus Unbound*, the declaration of faith of Prometheus: "Pain is my element as hate is thine." This **allusion** also emphasizes how small and pitiful Kamante was compared with Prometheus. The fact that Dinesen romanticizes Kamante reminds the reader of her belief in romanticism as she concludes that Kamante expected nothing but suffering, had no pity, and was prepared for the worst.

Missions: symbolism

Religious missions that claimed to be representations of truth and the good of their people are not presented as such by Dinesen. She makes it clear that she does not sympathize with the Missions yet was still friendly to them. Ironically, as Dinesen brings out, the French and Scotch Missions, both preaching love of fellow men, were hostile to each other.

The French Fathers are seen as ungenuine about their personal cause as they are about the Natives' cause, but they find time to lunch with Dinesen, quote the French author La Fontaine, and give advice on coffee planting. The Scotch Mission, apparently, represents and symbolizes blindness, "as if it could see nothing itself." Their major concern was changing Natives, not helping them. Dinesen states, ironically, that they worked hard to get African Natives into European clothes. But they had a hospital and this is where Kamante went for three months to be "cured."

Kamante as a symbol of Christianity

Miraculously cured of the running sores that had covered his thin legs, he returns from the Mission three months later "saved," a Christian, on Easter Sunday. Just as Christ arose from the dead, so Kamante comes to live (having been dead) with Dinesen because he is now like her, a Christian, and he attaches his fate to hers. Another example of Kamante as a Christ figure is Dinesen's comparing his talent for making things light to the legend of Christ who formed birds of clay and told them to fly. Kamante's perception of God in reality is distorted, as is evident in his mistaken impression of a grass fire as God's coming.

Characterization: minor character

Charles Bulpett of Nairobi is Dinesen's thermometer of Kamazte's culinary genius. An appropriate choice, Bulpett, a friend of Dinesen, symbolizes another era, since he is described as being an English gentleman of the Victorian age. Because he is a great traveler who has been all over the world and who has tasted everything, he was the person Dinesen felt the most pleasure dining with. His swimming the Thames and the Hellespont was an indication of how he fit Dinesen's idea of a hero and how he was linked to the great Romantic Lord Byron.

Contrast

The Natives' view of dining traditions is contrasted with the Europeans'. Food was survival for Natives, not the social event Europeans made of it. Kamante tolerated Dinesen's teaching of food - setting and other European traditions, but could never get the order of courses straight. The **irony** of his culinary art is that he felt contempt for it and did not eat what he cooked; if he tasted it at all, it was with distrust. Despite conversion to Christianity and connection with civilization, in his heart he was still a Kikuyu, preferring the maize cobs and roasted sweet potatoes of the Kikuyu tradition, and viewing his Msabu's fuss about food as crazy.

THE SAVAGE IN THE IMMIGRANT'S HOUSE

Title

The immigrant is Dinesen, and the savage, Kamante.

Setting

Rain, seen as a life - or - death phenomenon of Nature, is used to set the tone and mood for this section. What may have been taken for granted by Dinesen before is now appreciated through her understanding of rain and the Natives' being at its mercy. The passivity of the Natives during a time of crisis, compared with her complaining, accentuates their ability to communicate through silence and stillness. Drought was something to live with and endure as the forefathers has done. Dinesen observes their silence under the drought, realizing all the while that the Natives' very existence is at stake.

Analogical language

Dinesen uses personification and other forms of figurative language to convey the anticipation of rain. The urgency for rain and the preoccupation with its final arrival is conveyed in terms of Nature's sky. The night sky with the stars out of the way appeared to be "pregnant with benefaction" but its only charitable donation was the wind, not rain; which made it seem like punishment "as if the Universe was turning away from you," and you "being in disgrace with the Great Powers." The longing for rain is seen as reminiscent of a lover's embrace.

Dinesen - storyteller

Though she usually took to writing when times were dull on the farm, in this section Dinesen writes as a means of escape from the agony of waiting. Since she could not be "still" like the Natives, in the evening she wrote stories, fairy tales, and romances to keep her mind off her troubles, keep it somewhere "way off to other countries and times." The Natives, not understanding her reasons for writing, thought of the book she was working on as salvation, a "last attempt to save the farm." They would stand for long periods of time watching a work's progress, as though it was a ritual to guarantee rain.

Theme reprise: nature and civilization

Contrasting the Native world with her own, Dinesen found the boundary between her house and the outside to be passable. Little boys that let sheep and goats graze on her lawn make the link between her "civilized house and the life of the wild." The central (and most puzzling) symbol of civilization to them was an old German cuckoo - clock. All year round, they could tell time just by looking at the sun! It was such a fascinating event for the children big and small that their anticipation of the cuckoo's appearance is described as "a great movement of ecstasy," some Natives actually believing the cuckoo was alive. Another symbol of civilization was the typewriter which the houseboys watched to see how it worked.

Contrast and conflict

The conflict that exists in this story is one of contradictory religious beliefs, or, more importantly, what the teachings of the

Scotch Mission were in relationship to the Catholic teachings. Kamante, a converted Christian, had already formulated his beliefs which Dinesen's attempt to catechize him would not change. He could not understand that there were severe differences in the beliefs of Presbyterians and Catholics - both Christians. Was he being more ironic than Dinesen knew?

Contrast

Dinesen discovers the lack of prejudice on the part of the Natives to be somewhat remarkable, since the Europeans are guilty of being prejudiced against the Natives. Though prejudice may have been expected from primitive people, Dinesen concludes that the Natives have had myriad opportunities to acquaint themselves with other races and tribes. Their receptivity to new ideas makes "the Native more of a man of the world" than Europeans, settlers or missionaries.

Characterization

Kitau, Sheik ali Bin Sulin, Lewali of the Coast - all these characters offer the reader an idea of how Christian beliefs compare with or differ from Moslem culture and traditions. Kitau, a new servant from the Kikuyu Reserve, is revealed as meditative, observant, attentive, and in conflict over a choice of religion: Christian or Mohammedan? The reader learns that the Mohammedan will eat meat only of an animal whose throat was cut by a Mohammedan, to insure that the orthodox manner of slaughter was employed. It is a very touching moment of character study when Shereef assures Farah and Ismail that Dinesen, a disciple of Jesus Christ, in the name of God will make her bullets equivalent to the knife of an orthodox Mohammedan. Hence they could eat the meat of what she shoots. This incident is contrasted with Dinesen's taking Kamante to Mass.

Taking Kamante to a Christmas mass did in fact qualify Dinesen to be called "a disciple of Jesus Christ" since she promised him protection and exposed him to a celebration of Christ's birth. After overcoming his initial fear of the church, he appeared more comfortable with snakes and with the carrying of Knudsen's body. It is an interesting point in Dinesen's characterization of him that then he could scorn his "backward" kinsmen and boast about the power of God.

Biblical allusion

Dinesen's reference to the tale of Hagar's son dwelling with God in the wilderness and becoming an archer reflects her own desire to "grow" from being in the wilderness. The fact that Kamante asks if the gun was the Christian way and Dinesen shows him the Bible illustration reminds the reader of Dinesen's belief in Nature. She has chosen to use the "tools" of Nature: to become the archer and leave the "uncivilized" gun for the bow. Kamante's comment, "he was like you," makes it clear that this association with Nature is what Dinesen aspires to. And to the reader aware of mythology, the Natives' goddess Dinesen resembles here the Greek goddess of the hunt, Artemis (and the Roman goddess Diana, also an archer).

Foreshadowing and suspense

"The Savage in the Immigrant's House" ends with Kamante's cure of sick animals. He appears saint - like in his caring for them. Kamante could be compared to the Christian saint, Francis of Assisi, who earned the affection of animals and birds. This information about Kamante foreshadows his charge of another animal, and suspense is created by the name "Lulu" which makes the reader want to turn the page.

Characterization by allusions: Knudsen

One of Dinesen's finest portraits is her depiction of Knudsen. That he petitioned her for shelter reinforces our image of her as a feudal lord. That he regarded her as an authority figure, sometimes as a matriarch to be avoided, characterizes this blind old man as an incorrigible boy at heart. He believed in the legends of his mighty past and died still cherishing them. He always spoke of his great exploits in the third person in order to impose a mighty figure on the listener's mind and to obscure the real, bent old man who was really there. Dinesen's insightful perception of two individuals in one old body is made clear by her contrasting what he says, looks like, and what he was actually like. He needed a lot of attention and mistrusted women as those beings that stopped little boys as old as he from having their fun. Knudsen, like Esa in a previous section, is a representation of the natural cycle of life and death and fate.

Dinesen supplements her direct descriptions of Knudsen with three telling allusions: He "has the soul of a Berserk." In Scandinavian mythology, a Berserk is a wild, ferocious, warlike being often possessed of supernatural fury. When Dinesen finds it difficult to make Knudsen stop talking and go away, she alludes first to the *Ancient Mariner*. This is Samuel Taylor Coleridge's narrator in the poem named after him, a terrifying old man who keeps a wedding guest from attending the ceremony while the Mariner recites a long tale of supernatural adventure at sea.

OUT OF AFRICA

Then she alludes to the Old Man of the Sea, a character in *The Arabian Nights* who climbs on the shoulder of Sinbad the Sailor and refuses to get off.

A GAZELLE

Title

A gazelle is a small antelope noted for its graceful movements and lustrous eyes.

Lulu: parallel

Lulu, another wild animal that Dinesen brings up in her home, like Kamante, represents her links with the wilderness. Dinesen's descriptions move from nature to civilization and vice versa. Lulu, like Kamante, has qualities that supposedly are highly regarded in civilization: grace and the elegance of a princess.

Setting

The description of the Mysterious Forest creates the fairy - tale aspect of what will be Lulu's story. Dinesen paints the landscape with her magic wand, accentuating color and the secretiveness of the forest implied by a visitor's not being able to see the sky.

Analogical language

Dinesen's figurative language helps the reader to sense the forest, to expect that anything could happen here in this strange play of lights. Thus the grey fungus hangs from the trees "like long drooping beards" and a Giant Forest Hog is actually pictured as "a family man."

Lulu the Pearl: symbolism

Lulu represents an exiled princess from the wild. She is described in divine terms, and personified as having "all the air of a young Chinese lady," who stands on her "divine rights." She is anthropomorphized as the found princess of a fairy tale. Enjoying the freedom of Dinesen's house, Lulu symbolizes the total union of Dinesen's farm and the African landscape.

Cultural allusions

Lulu, the bushbuck fawn, looks to Dinesen like a "minutely painted illustration to Heine's song of the wise and gentle gazelles by the flow of the river Ganges." This **allusion** to Heinrich Heine, the great German Romantic poet, enhances Lulu's beauty and uniqueness. The **allusion** to Hera, the supreme goddess of Greek mythology, explains why Lulu doesn't wink and her eyes are without expression. The historical references to France's King Louis Philippe and the Duke of Orleans are used to minimize her meanness as not really being meanness at all.

Metamorphosis

Dinesen's depiction of Lulu as an epiphany crumbles as she witnesses Lulu's metamorphosis. The change in Lulu is expressed in Dinesen's description of the change of the environment.

There were **foreshadowing** hints of Lulu's not being gentle, but having the devil in her. Dinesen was unaware that the "war-dance" Lulu performs is really the female biological force which makes her appear crazy with frustration. Dinesen's response to Lulu's behavior when she appears to be satanic is a paean of praise in an attempt to see her in some realm of realism.

Linkage of chapters

We see now why Dinesen linked the first four chapters under the heading "Kamante and Lulu." These two creatures jointly symbolize the penetration of her lifestyle by the African man and the African animal. The union of all life, the blending of appearances, is consummately expressed in Dinesen's paradoxical conclusion that Lulu the antelope is Beauty and Kamante the man is Beast.

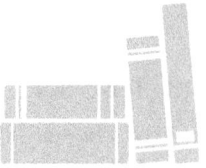

OUT OF AFRICA

TEXTUAL ANALYSIS

PART II: A SHOOTING ACCIDENT ON THE FARM

Structure. The incidents and reflections of Part II, like those of Part I, seem to be developed by the narrator's free associations. Part II, however, is more tightly organized around one single event, its consequences and its implications. Part II reads like a novella, with strong buildup of suspense; with conflicts between European values and African tribal values, and between the Natives themselves; and with a clear, sober, tragicomic resolution.

THE SHOOTING ACCIDENT

Structure

This dramatic chapter is formed in three parts, developing three successive and contrasting moods: The outdoor peace of the African night; the indoor horror of the shooting accident in a kitchen crowded with children; and the narrator's morning escape from the Elders into a solitary perspective.

Metaphor, comparisons, and contrasts

The ideas and situations in this famous piece of splendid writing are developed largely by comparisons and contrasts. The African night is when people come alive out of doors and enjoy the greatness of the sky, but the European night is when people withdraw from Nature and don't even know the phases of the moon. Night outdoors in Africa is like a dream, with the dreamers enjoying all the freedom of wish - fulfillment. Although Dinesen never mentions Freud or Jung, the fact is that her linking of night to the unconscious is solid depth psychology.

Dinesen's feeling that being "out" in the African night is like being "inside" a great Catholic cathedral, with its "companionability" and inclusive communal comforts, is a stroke of genius. Protestants can't be happy over her description, by contrast, of their churches as "business-like," but the comparison has often been made in literature, although rarely so well (in Richard Wilbur's poetry, for example). To this main **metaphor** of Africa's night as the nave of a cathedral, Dinesen adds many **metaphors** about details, like her description of the bats "cruising as noiselessly as cars on asphalt" and of particular constellations as a "doorkeeper" or jewels.

From pastoral to realistic prose

Dinesen must be credited with another tour de force in style when she goes abruptly from the pastoral mood, the wish-fulfillment dream, to the realistic mode, almost nightmarish in intensity. On one page she is enjoying the beauty of night; on the next, literally wading in blood. Her description of the blood on the floor, of the wounds in one boy's face and in another's chest, are as "hardboiled" as any description in the crime fiction of Dashiell Hammett.

Suspense

Dinesen's control over suspense is masterful here. From the very first sentence - when she recites a date as though it is of **epic** importance - we feel that something big is developing. After the huge African night absorbs a single shot, we are impatient to learn its nature but the narrator can only reflect on its meaning. When Belknap arrives with the facts, we must endure her reflections on his character, and then her reflections on the state of her car and of her road, all before we finally get to the kitchen of carnage. The end of the chapter is also a postponement, as Dinesen eludes the Elders and we are left in suspense about what their attitudes, their actions, will be.

Biblical allusion

Tarshish is a trading center variously and vaguely mentioned several times in the Bible. The "fact" that its Kings, themselves, would bring gifts to the dreamer has indeed all the qualities of dream: of a faraway place, of exotic people, of vague suggestion.

RIDING IN THE RESERVE

Title

In this context, a reserve is a place dedicated to a special and exclusive use, in this case, an area reserved as a natural habitat for wild animals that can be hunted for sport or food.

Conflict: internal drama

This chapter is a remarkable example of dramatic tension achieved through the thoughts - the interior monologue - of the narrator. On the one hand, Dinesen is reluctant to serve as judge in a manslaughter case, especially since she disagrees with the basic principle of tribal justice. The Kyama, or Council of Elders, will not be interested in the motive for the shooting (a child's - play accident) but only in the result: a death, but a death that in African law is the same as a deliberate murder. In either case, the loss must be compensated for: so many sheep or camels for one life or one injury. We infer that she feels resentment too because the Elders are all men but they expect her, a woman, to be the final judge. On the other hand, she operates on the basis of the noblesse oblige principle: rank imposes obligations, and we can easily infer that she never questions her right to that rank.

Mythopoeia

A remarkable passage is that devoted to the Natives' powers of myth - making (what we call in literary criticism mythopoeia) and "brass - serpenting," as she calls a related process. The Natives size up a stranger and soon give him a name that sums up their myth about him. They called a good hunter, a man who needs only one bullet to kill a beast, "One Shot." They call Dinesen "Lioness" presumably because of her strength and capacity for direct action: she has met and killed a lion and other wild beasts. During these times she notices that the Natives (and even she herself) tend to seize on one prominent person as a "brass serpent." In the Bible (Numbers, 21), God tells Moses to erect a bronze serpent and to instruct any person suffering from a snake bite to stare at the bronze effigy until he recovers. In every crisis, Dinesen's Natives seek out one person to stare at or concentrate on as though that person is Moses' bronze serpent.

Similes

Notice that Dinesen continues to produce **similes** at a Shakespearean rate. For example, the gazelles come to the green places to graze and so "look like toy animals stood upon a billiard table."

WAMAI

Characterization by contrast

Dinesen gives us a superb portrayal of the two principal figures in the "trial" or Kyama. The father of the boy who fired the gun, Kaninu, is wealthy (with five wives) and known to Dinesen to engage in unscrupulous schemes. The father of the dead boy, Jogona, is a poor (one wife) but gay person. The Elders, it is clear, are out to "get" Kaninu, to strip him of his ill - gotten wealth. But Jogona cannot enter into such a scheme. Dinesen's narrative makes clear what the economic and social distinctions among the Kikuyu are, and how psychologically complex their legal procedures are. The conflicts at the Kyama have little to do with the dead child (and his lost killer) but much to do with greed, deceit, misrepresentation of facts, opportunism.

Biblical allusion

Dinesen uses an **allusion** to the Book of Genesis to describe how Jogona feels after Dinesen draws up a legal document for him. The document gives him a new status, it preserves his name, and he looks now the way Adam did when God "formed him out of the dust, ... and [he] became a living soul."

WANYANGERRI

Metaphor: epic simile

This chapter is rich in metaphoric language as Dinesen continues her story of the consequences of the shooting accident. The Matron at the hospital, where Wanyangerri is undergoing plastic surgery on his shot - away jaw, wears so much makeup that Dinesen likens her to the Russian doll Katinka. This type of wooden doll can be unscrewed to reveal "another doll inside ... and another inside that." Wanyangerri himself emerges from surgery with a face that "looked ... like the head of a lizard," with no chin. Meanwhile the boy Kabero, who fired the shotgun blast that killed Wamai and wounded Wanyangerri, is discovered to be living with the Masai nation, whom Dinesen likens to "a dying lion with his claws clipped."

Then Dinesen treats us to that specialty in the poet's toolbox, the epic **simile**. This involves not the brief kind of comparison we have noted above (people compared with doll, lizard, lion), but a long luxurious, extended comparison. She compares Kaninu's efforts to conceal Kabero's whereabouts to the efforts of adult gazelles and birds "to distract your attention from their young." This detailed, extended **simile** of Dinesen's ranks with any one of Homer's.

On Kabero, Dinesen lavishes three metaphors: He had left her farm a lamb and returned a leopard; he carries his head the

Masai way, as if presenting it to you "upon a tray"; he is "cold like a statue," to be seen but not seeing.

When Dinesen concludes the chapter, with an ominous passage in which she considers the sudden resurgence of witchcraft on the farm, she does so with a disturbing personification: "... it looked ugly, as if it had come up from an old grave to flatten its nose upon my windowpanes."

A KIKUYU CHIEF

Mood

This chapter brings Part II to a close with a combination of (1) comic relief and (2) emotional relief. Both are attributable to Chief Kinanjui, a commanding figure appointed by the British to rule 100,000 Kikuyu. (1) He makes the mistake of drinking a tall tumbler of Dinesen's blended liquors all in one gulp and passes out, in comic fashion, on the road, seemingly dead for a while. (2) He is instrumental in helping to close the case of Wainaina's son Wanyangerri versus Kaninu's son Kabero just when "nobody could stand it any longer." It is further proof of Dinesen's skills as a literary artist that she represents both moods, both types of relief, with great fidelity. Neither comic relief nor emotional resolution is easy to recreate in writing.

Characterization

King Kinanjui is one of Dinesen's most delightful creations. He is tall and broad, virile (with a whole village of wives and children), he lives as he pleases, snoring in public for example, and he descends from his American - made car with the true bearing of a king. Dinesen contrasts him with Farah, her chief servant, to characterize Farah as the sheepdog and Kinanjui as the old ram.

Comparison of two tribes

Comparison is one of Dinesen's most reliable techniques, as she proves again when she has Farah define the Somali and the Masai in terms of each other. (Of course these observations are Farah's opinions.) The Somali, Mohammedans, are religious, he says, while the Masai are decidedly unspiritual. The Somali are fastidiously clean, the Masai - not. The Somali attach importance to the virginity of the brides they offer, while the Masai do not care about such things. This contrast may characterize Farah more than he characterizes the tribes.

OUT OF AFRICA

TEXTUAL ANALYSIS

PART III: VISITORS TO THE FARM

Setting and overall function. Dinesen devoted Parts I and II mainly to the farm and the doings of its occupants and closest neighbors. In Part III she expands the setting and the dramatis personae (people of the drama) to include visitors from other parts of British East Africa, from Europe and even Asia, and concludes symbolically with her airplane flights over Africa.

Epigraph and use of Latin. Dinesen's Latin epigraph for Part III - "Post Res Perditas" (After Things Lost) - promises us a return to normal life after the tragic events of Part II. Note that the very first paragraph of Part III will also use a Latin phrase, and that the very next sentence after it refers to Denys Finch - Hatton [sic]. The proximity of his name to the Latin expressions is appropriate. He taught Dinesen most of the Latin she knew. Our use here of the Latin sic (thus) indicates that we are writing "Finch -Hatton" as Dinesen herself wrote it, although her form was not correct. His actual family name is not hyphenated: Finch Hatton.

BIG DANCES

Use of Latin and metaphor

Dinesen promises us another highly metaphoric passage as she opens with the comparison of a friend who visits the house to "a heavenly messenger, who brings the panis angelorum," that is, the bread of angels. She uses **similes** to help us visualize the people and the setting. The Kikuyu dancers, when rubbed all over with chalk, "look ... like statues cut in rock" (a **simile** she converts into pure **metaphor** when she refers to their "limestone heads"). The old women open their mouths wide "like crocodiles." The overall scene, with its vast movements of bodies, is likened to a painting of a vast battle "observed from an eminence." The small fires that outline the dancing area are "like a circle of stars," and the stir of surprise that moves through the Kikuyu as the Masai approach sounds like the wind when it "blows through a bed of rushes." Dinesen is one of the most metaphoric writers in world literature. Thinking metaphorically involves the rare talent for seeing the similarity in dissimilars and using it to surprise and enlighten the reader.

Structure: topic sentences

This chapter is a perfect example of Dinesen's highly logical form, a perfect artistic contrast to her highly psychological use of **metaphor** (which appears to us as free association). She outlines her structure for us by using topic sentences, that is, sentences that tell us what a paragraph is all about. A topic sentence is usually the most generalized statement in the paragraph.

Note that the topic sentence of the introductory paragraph - "We had many visitors to the farm" -actually serves as a topic sentence for the whole chapter. The topic sentence of the next paragraph gives Finch - Hatton as one example of "visitors." The next topic sentence brings us to the main subject, the masses of visitors who attended the Ngomas or Native dances.

Then the main body of the chapter is divided up by topic sentences that indicate what happens at daytime Ngomas as distinguished from nighttime dances. One topic sentence is so important that it stands by itself introducing the concluding **episode**: "At one of the night Ngomas a dramatic incident took place."

Structure: contrasts

Dinesen again makes abundant use of contrasts to structure her material. Thus the "flighty beauties" of the city are contrasted with the "honest" girls of the farm, the day's dances with the night's, and the happy dancing of the Kikuyu alone with the tragic dancing after they are joined by the Masai.

Sense appeal

Most beginning writers give us mainly visual clues to what's going on. A professional like Dinesen works deliberately to exercise our other senses. Sounds play a major role in this chapter, as we hear the stamping feet, the clamor from the onlookers, the shrill shrieks of the girls. Dinesen's use of sound reaches a **climax** when she tells us that it was the drum and flute music that so entranced the faraway Masai that they were drawn, almost against their will, to join the Ngoma.

Historical allusion

Dinesen so wants us to understand the intensity of her talks with Denys that she compares them with the discussions two thirteenth - century saints had in Umbria, Italy, discussions that - so legend has it - lighted up the house. Saint Francis, founder of the Franciscan religious order, inspired Saint Clare to found a separate community for women so they could also live according to the Franciscan code.

"No sense ... for contrasts"

In a rather obscure sentence, Dinesen says the Natives have no "taste for contrasts." From context we can infer that she means they do not oppose themselves to Nature, as does the white man, who treats his environment as an enemy. While the white man sees himself and Nature as polar opposites, the Native sees himself and all other creatures as parts of Nature's continuum.

A VISITOR FROM ASIA

This short chapter is a perfect specimen of gentle but suspenseful narration and of effective characterization.

Two - way introduction

Dinesen opens with a transition that refers back to the Ngomas chapter as local in character, and forward to a different kind of visitor, from an exotic distance.

Narration

Dinesen begins her sketch proper as though it's a fairy tale: "There was in Nairobi... ." She builds suspense as she explains the strange (to her) customs attendant upon a visit by an Indian High Priest, her hesitation to accept the conditions set forth by the timber merchant, Farah's anxiety over her hesitation, then her consent followed by her forgetting to be there when the Priest arrives. She feeds our curiosity further with her description of the elegant entourage of four carts with six priests in each, and with the realization that hostess and High Priest can communicate only through pantomime. The situation reaches its **climax** when she decides to add to the "sham gift" a real gift of her own choice, thus ending a situation in which she had been assigned a role by taking the initiative and staging a surprise event. The ending too is a surprise, with the silent pantomime resulting, months later, in a totally unexpected development.

Characterization

The portrait of the High Priest is charming, colorful, and sensitive. He does not need to speak his hostess' language, or she his, for his aura of spirituality, which he casts over the material world too, communicates all he stands for. He has found safety and security through acceptance of circumstances, a strong **theme** for Dinesen herself.

We must see her description of his face - "that of a very young infant" - in the Romantic context. To the Romantics, the child is closer to God and to Truth, to intuition and insight, than the adult is.

Allusion to art

Likening the High Priest to some "noble infant, some old Master's child Jesus," Dinesen was probably thinking of the Christ Child and Madonna as painted by Raphael, Bonsignori, or Parmigianino. She herself was a painter.

Dinesen's prejudice

The one flaw in this sketch is Dinesen's petulant remark that "there are times when colored people cannot make themselves clear to save their lives." In a more objective moment she might have realized that "there are times when oppressed people don't want to make themselves clear to their rulers," when lack of candor is their last vestige of dignity, maybe their one way to save their lives.

THE SOMALI WOMEN

This chapter is distinguished by its tone, its swift characterization of groups as well as of individuals, its neat social judgments, and its rich use of **allusions** and metaphor.

Structure

So casually does this chapter develop that we're tempted to think it happens by free association. Actually, the chapter follows an overall plan. It starts with Farah's marriage and ends with the birth of his son, but it focuses during that period on "his women."

And that chronological account also accommodates Dinesen's personal views on the position of women, Somali and European.

Tone

Dinesen's attitude toward her subject is one of gentle bemusement, verging on **satire**, over the paradoxes in the life of the Somali women. The **irony** begins in the first sentence, when she declares she "cannot write much" about them "for they would not" like that. Then she proceeds to write a thorough though compact estimate of their predicament, at times humorous but in a tragicomic way…. like it or not.

Allusions

Dinesen makes many of her points by alluding to biblical, mythological, and literary characters and, in one case, to Danish sculpture. Although Farah's household already included his wife, her sister, their mother, and a girl cousin, he took in an orphan girl, so Dinesen thinks, "after the pattern of Mordecai and Esther." That is, Farah hoped to command a good price for her when she reached the marriage age. In The Book of Esther, in Hebrew Scripture, Mordecai raises an orphan girl and succeeds in having her chosen as the queen of the Persian king.

Dinesen uses the Bible again to make a point about the cousin, from whom the author "learned the true paraphrase of the story of Joseph and Potiphar's wife." In Genesis, in both the Old Testament and the Koran, Joseph is working for Potiphar whose wife makes advances to Joseph. He flees but loses his cloak in the process, she shows it to her husband as evidence that Joseph has propositioned her, and he is a cast into prison.

Dinesen is coy about revealing just what the "true paraphrase" was, but from the context we can infer it stressed female victory over a male, or maybe even included "much frankness" about the physical details.

To describe the way Farah's mother - in - law gave advice, Dinesen says she uttered it "in Sibylline fashion." The Sibyls were prophetesses in the ancient world whose prophecies were supposed to be divinely inspired but were not always easy to interpret. And Dinesen describes the girls as having reputations "as fresh as Dian's visage." Diana was the Roman goddess of the moon, or the moon herself, with clear complexion and absolute chastity.

Farah's sisters-in-law, Dinesen says, were "the glass of fashion and the mold of maidenly form," Dinesen's adaptation of Ophelia's description of Hamlet. By comparing Farah's in - laws with these great characters in world literature, Dinesen belittles them and their petty concerns.

The **satire** is rounded out with Dinesen's (rather cruel) account of how the cousin, a Mohammedan, fell in love with a postcard picture of a statue of Christ in the Cathedral of Copenhagen. The statue is the work of Albert Bertel Thorvaldsen, a Danish neoclassicist sculptor (1970–1844).

Feminist basis for the satire

Dinesen, we must remember, was a feminist, and that in a day when feminism was an unfulfilled dream. In a day when this was "a man's world," she managed a business with hundreds of employees, she undertook wartime field - operations of great danger, she hunted wild animals and gave first aid to bloodied victims of gunfire. In short, she did everything, vocationally and avocationally, that a man could do and that usually was considered man's work or man's play.

Hence her bemusement at the predicament of the Somali women, who actually were owned outright by men (fathers, brothers, or husbands) and yet acted as though they were the conquerors of their men. The position of woman in Somali society reminded Dinesen of that of "the ladies of a former generation in my own country." But many readers, male as well as female, can well wonder why Dinesen found these victims of male domination more an object of ridicule than of sympathy.

Analogical language

To describe "Farah's women," Dinesen resorts again to the animal world for her comparison: they make up a "gentle flight of dusky doves." And since their extorting fine clothes from their men is part of their sexual strategy, Dinesen says they wear them "like conquered banners."

Characterization

The Somali women are characterized, in short, as constantly mindful of the price they can command on the marriage market, creatures who enjoy stories in which the heroine outwits the hero but who in real life are totally dependent on and subservient to their male masters. The sarcasm with which Dinesen treats the Somalis carries over to other people in the story. When Dinesen asks the French missionaries, for example, if she can bring the

Mohammedan women to their mission, she says "The French Fathers [were] pleased that something was going to happen."

OLD KNUDSEN

Structure: introduction

Note that Dinesen carefully relates each chapter introduction to the overall title of Part III. The first four chapters have each opened with an outright reference to visitors: (1) "We had many visitors," (2) "Visitors from distant countries as well," (3) "Of one group of visitors," and now (4) "Sometimes visitors from Europe drifted into the farm... ." After reminding us of her overall topic of "visitors," she then, in each case, briefly distinguishes the visitors in that chapter from visitors in the others.

Structure: internal

Once her chapter subject is related to, and distinguished from, other chapter subjects, Dinesen relies often on topic sentences to indicate the direction of her content. We know that she is moving from charcoal burning to building a pond because she announces the new topic in the very first sentence of a new paragraph. But she also divides charcoal burning and dam-building into subtopics and introduces each of these as well with a topic sentence.

Dinesen's overall plan for this chapter is to characterize Knudsen, as one of the European visitors and as an individual, by catching him at work on these projects and recalling how and what he talked about during his work.

Structure: contrast

As we have often noted, Dinesen often structures by contrast. After describing Knudsen's wailing, sneering, supervising, his active postures and movements, she then pictures his corpse, quiet and passive, being tossed about in a car.

Structure and content

Having set up a tight and formal structure, Dinesen than feels free to follow her free associations.

Tone and self - characterization

As in her chapter on the Somali women, Dinesen adopts again a satirical tone, in this case involving outright mockery of Knudsen. This attitude of hers creates a tension because, we finally realize, she also admires Knudsen. Here is a major factor in her self - characterization: She is prone to ridicule the very things she admires. These are, in Knudsen's case, his aristocratic indifference to law and **convention**, his life as an outcast from a European society that she too dislikes, his talents as an engineer transforming Nature to suit his purposes. Her very last sentence at last acknowledges this bond between them: "... I was ... a brother."

Characterization: Knudsen

But, in a very brilliant analysis of his character, Dinesen first found herself a mother - figure before she became "a brother." Knudsen is a refugee from women. Dinesen dramatizes this very effectively: When she suspects that his plan for getting fish is to steal them, he slinks away, caught again by a mother - figure, confirmed again in his suspicion that women spoil all the fun. But all this belittling of him cannot conceal the fact that he is capable of engineering vast enterprises. We feel a bit sorry for him when Dinesen makes an all - too - easy point by comparing him with Noah and then sees Knudsen as "content in the thought that everybody but himself was soon to drown." In "The Somali Women," Dinesen mocked women with aspirations to matriarchy; here she mocks patriarchy too.

Allusion: Puck

Perhaps a fairer comparison appears in this **simile** about Knudsen: "like a Puck grown old and blind and very malicious." Originally Puck was an evil demon in popular folklore. Shakespeare popularized him as a merry, mischievous sprite. Dinesen ages him back to the evil demon.

Diction

Typical of Dinesen's love of the unusual word is her sentence " ... charcoal - burners ... are given to poetry and taradiddle." Taradiddle consists of little lies and pretenses. This sentence foreshadows Knudsen's taradiddle when he decides that their charcoal - burning could not succeed because they had no snow at hand.

Sensuous detail and metaphor

Earlier we commented on how Dinesen adds to visual details significant auditory details. Here we should note too how she adds olfactory details: "the cut wood smelt like gooseberries; ... the piercing, fresh, rank, sour smell of the burning kiln was as bracing as a sea breeze." The **simile** linking kiln smell to sea breeze is just one of her steady stream of "bracing" analogies: Note that the charcoal is the "little mummy of the wood" and the row of new ponds is "like pearls upon a string."

A FUGITIVE RESTS ON THE FARM

Structure: fairy tale

The key words now that introduce the second of the "visitors from Europe" are "one traveler" and the catchword in the title: A Fugitive. After this logical tieback to the overall category of "Visitors to the Farm," Dinesen uses the simple chronology of the fairy tale.

Dramatic structure

Within this seemingly simple chronology there is a superbly crafted drama of reversal. Drama exploits the difference between appearance and reality. At the beginning maitre d'hotel Emmanuelson is so oily and talkative that Dinesen changes over to another hotel dining - room just to avoid him. Then he is so shabby, so unkempt, so rundown when she finds him at her doorstep that she decides she will not grant him the room and board overnight that he needs. Those are the appearances that he has to fight against.

Step by step Dinesen shows how he wins her over: his courtesy; his appreciation of a fine wine; his real profession, acting, which he cannot practice in Kenya; his confession of his faith: "... with the exception of God I believe in absolutely nothing... ." These aspects of his character shine through the appearances and hint at nobler realities. They change her mind, and her new openness to him makes possible still other revelations of reality. The ending is a triumph for both of them.

Dramatic irony

As one of his unwitting mistakes that he has to overcome, Emmanuelson urges her to read aloud with him *Ghosts* by Henrik Ibsen. This is a play about the effects of hereditary syphilis on the wife and son of a syphilitic husband. Nothing could have tried Dinesen's patience more: she was herself the daughter of one syphilitic man and the wife of another. Emmanuelson's acting in ignorance of these facts is a superb instance of dramatic **irony**, a situation in which one or more characters and the audience are privy to facts unknown to the speaker of the moment.

Symbolism of Emmanuelson's repertoire

Notice that in addition to the role of the son Oswald in *Ghosts*, Emmanuelson has played Armand Duval in *La Dame aux Camelias* by Alexander Dumas fils. Armand loves Camille, an ex-courtesan, who is persuaded by his family to give him up. They are reunited only at her death bed. These roles of the victim of circumstances are symbolic of Emmanuelson's own tragic life. Dinesen has described him as a man who differs "in his tastes and ideas of the pleasures of life, from the customary." The brilliant critic Robert Langbaum suggests that Emmanuelson's tragic secret - the reason for his being a fugitive - is that he was a homosexual.

Themes

The outcast, even sometimes the outlaw, are portrayed as heroic by Dinesen. She completely understands why the Masai take Emmanuelson in and provide him with safe conduct through wild territory. The true aristocrat and the true proletariat, she says, are both capable of understanding tragedy. But the bourgeois deny tragedy, they sweep it under the rug. And so the artist Emmanuelson is a fugitive from middle-class society but a welcome guest among the Masai. (The poet William Butler Yeats also saw an affinity between the aristocracy and the working class: They both have individual style, in contrast to the middle class which prefers conformity.)

Theatre as metaphor

Notice that once Emmanuelson is revealed to be an actor, the metaphors are theatrical. For example, he plans now to be his own prompter, a wonderful **metaphor** for someone taking over full responsibility for one's performance in life.

VISITS OF FRIENDS

Overall structure and title phrase

Notice that the title, repeated in the opening phrase, distinguishes the visitors of this chapter from those in earlier chapters of Part III: friends as distinct from acquaintances. Notice too the careful design: Her five chapters devoted to casual contacts have served as an emotional buildup to the next three chapters devoted to her more profound relationships.

Internal structure

Dinesen designs every chapter according to its functions. This chapter seems structured to answer broad preliminary questions like How, Why, Who, What, and When, the Where being mainly understood. Notice that these six questions are the basis of the journalist's "lead," also called the "five W's and an H." Then notice how she alternates between broad answers and detailed examples. Here is such a rough outline as Dinesen herself might have used:

- How "the farm knew" that "visits of my friends were happy events in my life"

2 examples: the young Masai the Squatter Toto

- Why my wanderer friends were eager to visit

Details: books, linen sheets, atmosphere, home cooking, etc. Examples of dialogue by Denys and Berkeley

- How I prepared for their visits

Details: recipes, European plants Anecdote: 12 peony - bulbs

- Who the friends are: vignettes

Hugh Gustav Ingrid (Ingrid's houseboy and Farah: counterpoint.) Mrs. Thompson Old Mr. Bulpett Threesome: Bulpett, Denys, me

The Peony parable

The moral to this anecdote is at least twofold: (1) Impatience for immediate results can destroy all chance of long - term benefits. (2) We must cooperate with Nature by respecting her requirements. In addition to illustrating the ways Dinesen tried to make her European friends happy (by having European flowers for them to smell), this anecdote - parable also tells us a great deal about how to cultivate friends.

Technical challenge

The biggest technical challenge in this chapter was the Who. It's as though Dinesen is to take us on a quick tour of a portrait gallery. Which details should she stress in each case that would make the portrait memorable? She succeeds with a combination of physical appearance, mannerisms, eccentricities, topics the person talks about, and her continuing reliance on **metaphors** as well as literary and cultural allusions.

Characterization: Hugh Martin

His physique is quickly pictured with a **simile**: He looks like a "fat Chinese idol." His cultural breadth, his knowledge of people, his philosophy are all suggested by the use of literary allusions. He calls Dinesen "Candide," after the hero of Voltaire's philosophical novel Candide. As the name suggests, Candide is honest, naive in the best sense of being without bias, being open to new experience. In return, Dinesen calls him "Doctor Pangloss," after Candide's tutor.

Characterization: Gustav Mohr

He is characterized by a **simile**: he arrives on the farm "like a stone out of a volcano;" by his social attitude: he believes farmers must help each other; by his compulsive talking: on subjects including Knut Hamsun and the Bible. Hamsun was a Norwegian novelist who focused, first, on the inner turmoil of the hero and, later, on society's effects on the individual - both passionate concerns of Mohr.

Characterization: Ingrid Lindstrom

She is distinguished as another woman farmer with whom Dinesen could empathize, by her "weather - beaten face" and the strong white teeth of a "laughing Valkyrie." By this **allusion** Dinesen probably means not the old bloodthirsty maidens of Old Norse legend, but one of the Wagnerian Valkyries, lusty and wise Amazonian types.

Counterpoint: Ingrid's cook

As counterpoint to the Ingrid - Karen friendship, Dinesen offers the relationship between Ingrid's cook, Kemosa, and Karen's superintendent, Farah. (Notice that by now Dinesen has used the word slave three times in two pages to describe the way Mohr helped her, the way Ingrid worked to save her farm, and the way Kemosa toils for Ingrid. Apparently, in Dinesen's time and place, keeping alive on the frontier was hard work.)

Characterization: Mrs. Thompson

She is made memorable by Dinesen's selection of distinctive details: of a woman who lives for the pleasure of managing prize - winning horses who, when she learns she has only weeks to live, makes Dinesen a gift of her last acquisition, a prize - jumping pony who, like Thompson herself, lives only a few months longer. (Implicit in these portraits is the unstated fact that they include three women who led independent lives in "a man's world.")

Characterization: Old Bulpett

Dinesen characterizes him by the unusual things he does and says. For example, he has swum the Hellespont (the Dardanelles, a mile - wide strait), thus emulating Lord Byron who did it to emulate the classical hero Leander. And Bulpett makes a remark about liking to have wings that is subtly risque and so good Dinesen saves it for her punch - line: "I suppose I should think it over, though, if I were a lady."

THE NOBLE PIONEER

Genre, title, structure

While this chapter is an integral part of an autobiographical narrative, a prose pastoral, or a memoir, it can also stand by itself as a eulogy to "The Noble pioneer" of the title, and as a paean of praise of him in particular and of friendship in general.

Although it is not so formally organized as most other chapters, it does fall roughly into three parts:

(1) The first section is a tribute to a three - person friendship, including an explanation of why the three were attracted to each other and also were more acceptable to the Natives than other whites were.

(2) The second part is a tender but sometimes ironic account of the public services of Berkeley Cole as a pioneer and as an intermediary between white rulers and black subjects.

(3) The conclusion is an account and an explanation of the meaning of his death to his friends and to his public.

Themes

Form and content are so identical in this chapter that a statement of its **themes** sounds like a restatement of its structure. One formulation of its message could be:

(1) Close, intense friendship creates what Dinesen calls, in her opening sentence, "a communist establishment," with each friend giving according to his abilities and taking according to his needs (to paraphrase Karl Marx himself: *Criticism of the Gotha Programme*, 1875).

(2) The Industrial Age has thrown many valuable types of personalities into a state of exile, psychological and physical.

(3) War is absurd and ironic.

Characterization of a threesome

Dinesen says that what Berkeley Cole and Denys Finch - Hatton had in common was their alienation from Industrial Society. They were outcasts but were made to feel like deserters. Ironically, it was their alienation from European values that made them acceptable to the Natives and hence valuable to the Europeans as intermediaries with the Natives. And, as Langbaum points out, what Dinesen says about her two friends, we should say about all three friends: She has characterized herself as well as them.

Characterization: Berkeley Cole (1)

Dinesen characterizes Cole through a combination of (1) anecdote, (2) **allusion**, and (3) **metaphor**. The paragraph about his drinking "champagne in the forest" shows both his belief in living according to aristocratic ritual and the fact that each friend had a right to make demands on the others. The long narration of his wartime service shows how his "knowledge of, and friendships with, the Masai" resolved a delicate diplomatic situation in an astute and subtle way.

Characterization: Cole (2).

To further characterize Cole, Dinesen resorts to a stream of literary and historical **allusions** (many of them made possible by her other friend Denys' tutoring of her). Psychologically unfit for life in the Industrial Age, Cole was an atavist, that is, a "throwback" to earlier ages. Let us see how Dinesen's **allusions** suggest this. That he "could have walked in and out of" the English Court of Charles II (1630–1685) means he was witty, urbane, pleasure - loving, aristocratic. Indeed, we infer he was superior in wit to those great witty English dramatists, William Congreve (1670–1729) and William Wycherley (1640–1716). Cole's atavism made him seem sometimes rather ridiculously to be riding Rosinante, who was the steed of Cervantes' great atavistic hero, Don Quijoxte (1605). Cole might even have been tutored by Alexandre Dumas' brave and quick - witted hero, Charles d'Artagnan of *The Three Musketeers and Twenty years After* (the latter cited by Dinesen in French: *Vingt Ans Apres*).

Characterization: Cole (3)

Dinesen also uses two **metaphors** to characterize Cole. He was as quiet, as comfort - loving as a cat who makes others comfortable too. And like a cat, he had no principles, just prejudices, says Dinesen, in seeming contradiction to the impression she gives that he was noble. And what do you think of the last line of the chapter, in which his death is described metaphorically: "A cat had got up and left the room"? Does this image succeed in its purpose, or is it a letdown, a belittling of a person Dinesen really admires?

The greatest **metaphor** for Cole is, of course, Dinesen's point that his life and death were synonymous with the life and death of a period in colonial relations.

Absurdity of war

In her eulogy to Cole, Dinesen gives us two effective dramatizations of the absurdities of warfare: (1) Cole's servant and Dinesen's, working side by side in mutual respect for their masters, couldn't talk to each other because far away their two tribes were at war. (2) Cole had to reward the Native chiefs with medals but he couldn't pin them on naked men. And the medals bore the inscription The Great War for Civilization, highly ironic since it was really a war for colonies, including the colony in which the chiefs were now subjects to a foreign power.

Incidentally, the lines from Lord Byron's *The Waltz*, which Dinesen alludes to in her "distribution of medals" story, are misquoted. She was probably quoting from memory of a poem Finch - Hatton had recited to her. The actual lines are:

Yet still between his Darkness and his Brightness there passed a mutual glance of great politeness.

Characterization: Finch - Hatton

Since Dinesen sees Finch - Hatton too as an atavist, she follows through by suggesting the age in which he should have lived. Her saying that he could have "walked arm in arm" with Sir Philip Sidney and Sir Francis Drake means he was a Renaissance man, that is, the kind of well - rounded man the upper class admired in that day. Sidney (1554–1586) was a poet, a soldier, a scholar, and a courtier. (Like Dinesen, incidentally, Sidney wrote a prose pastoral: *Arcadia*.) Drake (1540–1596) was an explorer and a soldier who greatly expanded the horizons of the Elizabethan Age.

Non - characterization: Finch - Hatton

Reading this chapter and the next, moviegoers who have viewed Sydney Pollack's film *Out of Africa* will wonder why the book of that name does not depict Finch - Hatton as Dinesen's lover. The book *Out of Africa* is based on Dinesen's experiences in Africa but does not include all of them. For the purposes of her prose pastoral she selected only those autobiographical details strictly needed to ramify her pastoral themes. Pollack's *Out of Africa*, on the other hand, draws on several other works, including Dinesen's *Letters from Africa* and *Shadows on the Grass*; Judith Thurman's *Isak Dinesen: The Life of a Storyteller*; and Errol Trzebinski's *Silence Will Speak*.

WINGS

Structure, function, symbolism

This chapter serves as the highpoint for both Part III, "Visitors to the Farm," and for the entire book. This reaches the peak of Dinesen's happiness in Africa; after this point in the action the narrator's fortunes run downhill.

"Wings" is divided into three parts. (1) The first deals with the happiness and clarity that friendship and art bring into the narrator's life. (2) The second part dramatizes the happiness that hunting brings to a couple, and drives home another major **theme** in Dinesen's work. (3) The third section describes the thrill of flying and is placed at a symbolic point in the book. As the brilliant critic Robert Langbaum puts it, "The heaven to which she mounted with Denys makes the appropriate **climax** to the idyllic section of *Out of Africa*. For it was from that height, and largely from that airplane, that her happiness came crashing down in ruins around her."

Themes

(1) One major **theme** is stated at once in the poetic opening paragraph, which means, in effect, that a passionate friendship, such as the narrator has with Denys, illuminates and intensifies all of life and puts everything into proper focus and perspective. Note that in the light of this happy relationship, Dinesen learns the Hebrew, Greek, and Latin classics, and both classical and modern symphonic music.

(2) A second **theme** is the disappearance of oral storytelling from modern life and Dinesen's interest in reviving it. She develops her skills in this art under the invigorating influence of Denys. Note again how alienated he is from Europe and how attuned he is to Africa: He loves to hear stories narrated, an art now dead in Europe but still thriving in Africa.

(3) A passionate friendship brings "luck" to the friends. Hunting alone, Denys or Dinesen will have less luck than when hunting together. We can infer that this is true because their skills, attitudes, and awareness are all intensified by the personal harmony.

(4) Frei lebt wer sterben kann, German for He who can face death can live free. Dinesen the narrator says that Dinesen the character proposed a lion hunt to Denys by saying, "... let us go and risk our lives unnecessarily."

(5) A related motif, one that the present - day ecologist would abhor, is that the narrator "could not live" until she had "killed a specimen of each kind of African game." Today's critic would question why shooting the animal

on film might not be as nourishing. Was Dinesen, in her desire to be the equal of a man, sometimes more macho than even men should be?

(6) Another **theme** we can find in "Wings" is the nature of time. The European wants to speed up but the African wants to savor time. This contrast is beautifully expressed in the final anecdote. An old Kikuyu, when he learns that, when flying high, Denys and Dinesen still can't see God, wonders why they fly at all.

(7) Dinesen's implicit answer would be - or so we can infer from the rest of "Wings" - that flying provides an overview of earth and perspective on experience, both invaluable.

Narration via allusions

Notice how Dinesen uses **allusions** to other literature to extend and intensify the reader's experience of her own narrative. She says she "always thought I might have cut a figure at the time of the plague of Florence." This alludes to Giovanni Boccaccio's classic collection, *The Decameron* (1351–53). In the frame story, seven young ladies and three young gallants meet in a church in Florence, during the plague of 1348, and decide to escape to the Fiesole hills. There they while away the time telling stories, ten a day for ten days, a hundred novellas in all. In addition to letting us know that Dinesen feels she could have been one of those famous narrators, is our author also **foreshadowing** her Part IV, which is also a long collection of short pieces?

Next she tells us that to tell Denys a story, she would sit on the floor "cross - legged like Scheherazade herself." Here her ambitions are likened to those of the famous narrator of *The Arabian Nights' Entertainments* (also known as *A Thousand and One Nights*). Scheherazade actually saved her life by telling stories to her misogynist husband; Dinesen's telling stories to Denys was also lifegiving and life-determining for the great author-to-be.

Notice that Dinesen is thinking of *Arabian Nights* again when their flight from Lake Natron to Naivasha takes them, she realizes, along the path that the Roc, the giant bird in "Sinbad the Sailor," took.

Dinesen refers to the scene of the three dead animals as "the fifth act of a classic tragedy" because it was in the fifth act that dramatists from Seneca to Shakespeare resolved the problems of the play - often with the stage littered with corpses. Notice that *Out of Africa* is also in five parts, with her tragic resolution to come in Part V.

She refers to the lioness as the femme fatale because in literature we give that name to the dangerous female who lures men to their death (e.g., Bridget in Dashiell Hammett's *The Maltese Falcon*): The lioness caused the death of the giraffe, herself, and (posthumously) the lion.

Dinesen's reference to The Prophet and the Archangel Gabriel - which makes a brilliant parallel to her experience with the still-hot teapot - alludes of course to the Koran: Mohammed is the Prophet to whom Gabriel reveals the Word of God.

Sense appeal

Beginning writers, we have noted earlier, tend to communicate best the visual experiences of their characters, but professionals like Dinesen strive to recreate sensations of sound, smell, taste, and touch as well as sight. In this chapter Dinesen's recollections of life with Finch - Hatton bring back to her one glorious experience after another of all the senses wide open to physical reality.

Two passages especially deserve our careful study. The first records Dinesen's impressions on the flight to Lake Natron. Its shores smell sour and salty. The white lake bottom gives its water a clear azure color as it lies in the lap of the tawny earth. When they land on the shore, the sun leans on them so palpably hot it hurts.

The other is her famous tour - de - force description of the early morning highlands air as so tangibly cold and fresh that she feels the "flows of chilliness" across her face like "deep - sea currents." She develops the illusion that their car is riding on the sea bottom. Later "whirls of smells" drift past, a rank odor of olive bushes, a saline scent of burnt grass.

Characterization: Denys

This chapter adds to our earlier impressions of the Renaissance man. He is spontaneous, does only what he wants to do when he wants to, and earns enough money to guarantee himself those freedoms. He is a fearless hunter, able to drop a lion usually with one shot, at most two. ("Three shots, two lions!" the Natives shout.) He brings new adventures into Dinesen's life, mental explorations into Greek and Latin literature, physical thrills in an open - cockpit airplane. He is independent enough to find modern European industrial life distasteful, but he prefers modern music to Beethoven (perhaps because modern music is, like him, anti - bourgeois?).

Characterization: Dinesen

The author portrays herself as endlessly eager for new experiences, in love with music, literature, hunting, and flying; most alive when Denys is her guest. She respects his desire to be there only when he wants to, although she obviously wishes he were there more often. She enjoys her status as a baroness, her stewardship of "my people," and she clearly believes that rank has its responsibilities. She recalls without embarrassment a time when she just couldn't live until she had killed at least one of each kind of African game - animal. She believes that you can't live fully unless you're willing to risk death.

On some details we have to distinguish between what Dinesen the author tells us about her character named Dinesen, and what more objective writers tell us. Dinesen the author says that she shot one of the lions feeding on the giraffe. But Judith Thurman, Dinesen's biographer, says Denys killed both of them. Dinesen the author says that Denys had no other home in Africa except hers. Thurman refutes this. Dinesen was trying simply to enhance her story, for example, in the case of the killing of the lions, to give the story, as Thurman puts it, "more symmetry."

Freudian symbolism

Since Dinesen was, then, engaging in fantasy as well as fact when she recalled that lion hunt, we should add a Freudian observation: Her description of Denys' rifle takes on unacknowledged significance as a phallic symbol.

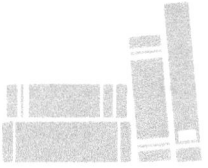

OUT OF AFRICA

TEXTUAL ANALYSIS

PART IV: FROM AN IMMIGRANT'S NOTEBOOK

....

FUNCTION IN OVERALL STRUCTURE

In the analogy of the five-act tragedy - which Dinesen herself has mentioned - Parts I to III would be the rising action and IV and V the falling action. So long as the **catastrophe** does finally occur in Part V, the author is free to make Part IV any kind of bridge or transition from rising to falling action. Sometimes, the dramatist uses Act IV for a final reaction, an incident in which it appears that the hero will reverse the downward trend in his fortunes and rise again.

Dinesen chooses to make Part IV a suspenseful plateau on which the resolution is simply postponed and we're made uncertain whether it will be a happy or a tragic one. Supposedly, she is now actually making us privy to some thirty - two sketches, vignettes, meditations, parables, etc., from a notebook kept in Africa. Some support **themes** already established in Parts I – III, others foreshadow the fall in Part V. But in almost every case, every "Note" is interesting in itself. It's as though we're watching some sideshows while we're waiting, during an intermission, for the main action to resume.

FICTION VS. AUTOBIOGRAPHY

Langbaum reports that Dinesen wrote all of *Out of Africa* after she had returned to Europe. So the implication that these Notes are from an actual notebook kept in Africa is a fictitious one. This is now one of several places where we have discovered that *Out of Africa* is only semi - autobiographical. Not only does it omit any autobiographical elements - e.g., the real relationship with Denys, the fact that brother Thomas Dinesen lived for a while on the farm - but it also creates several fictional elements, like Dinesen's killing a lion really shot by Denys, and Part IV being excerpts from an African notebook.

We shall here comment briefly on the **theme** of each Note, on the literary technique it employs to make its point, and on the connection with the rest of the book when that is not already obvious.

"THE WILD CAME TO THE AID OF THE WILD"

Apparently Dinesen sees this as a case of "poetic justice" A man who tries to subdue Nature is punished by Nature. One proud animal saves another from a fate worse than death (bondage). The title is mystical in its implication that the leopard is consciously "aiding" the ox, but Dinesen does see such patterns in Fate. It's a parable, i.e., a short story with a moral.

"THE FIREFLIES"

In addition to the excellent recreation of physical detail (the firefly in the hand turning the palm from flesh color to pale green), the main literary accomplishment is the way the sight of the fireflies in the woods becomes a fantasy of children dancing there with torches. Perception is subjective; the mind imposes images on reality.

"THE ROADS OF LIFE"

Message: The patterns that one's journeys make can't be understood until one can see them from an overview afterward (a **theme**, too, of "Wings"). The Latin line is from Virgil's *Aeneid*, an **epic** poem about Troy and Rome, and it means: A grief too heavy to be told, O queen, you ask me to renew. Can good (elegance, stateliness, tenderness) come out of suffering? This "moving picture" was a favorite story in the Dinesen nursery.

"ESA'S STORY"

The story illustrates the nature of luck and the way the powerful can use their legal power to bring illegal bad luck to the powerless. A neat literary device is Esa's use of Dinesen's remark about the overworked ox to explain his own predicament: an analogy. Notice that Dinesen places the concluding part of Esa's story much later in Part IV to give us a sense of time passing.

"THE IGUANA"

The moral seems to be: To possess something you want in its living state you might have to kill it. Note the parallel to "The Wild Came to the Aid of the Wild." Note too the effective **simile**: The Iguana's coloring is like the glow behind a church window or a comet's tail.

"FARAH AND THE MERCHANT OF VENICE"

Moral: Taken out of its original cultural context, a work of art can raise different questions in another culture. Because of the alleged litigiousness of his tribe, Farah sees different problems in Shakespeare's play than Shakespeare's English - speaking audience sees. Note the parallel to the Iguana story: Anything or person must stay in context in order to remain the same. (Is it possible Farah is being sarcastic, or pulling Dinesen's leg?)

"THE ELITE OF BOURNEMOUTH"

Moral: While the true aristocrat (like Dinesen and her close friends) feels noblesse oblige (rank gives one responsibilities), the pseudo - aristocrat feels that rank absolves him from social responsibilities. In the opinion of true aristocrats, the affluent middle-class person is just such a pseudo - aristocrat: his wealth and other advantages owe nothing to the community from which he extracted them.

"OF PRIDE"

In spite of its somewhat stuffy, pompous, and self - righteous tone, this little homily delivers some thought - provoking points. Most famous is Dinesen's definition of pride: "faith in the idea that God had, when he made us." Note the connection between our interpretation here of the "Elite" note above and Dinesen's definition of a good citizen as someone who "finds his happiness in the fulfillment of his duty to the community." This is Dinesen's concept of the true aristocrat as opposed to the selfish bourgeois.

"THE OXEN"

This animal fable, like all animal fables, is supposed to offer ideas we can transfer to the human condition. How many limits on our lives do we blame on "life, and the conditions of the world," because certain economic or political powers want us to? Which of our unfair burdens could be traced, like the oxens' burdens, to men themselves? Which forces in our environment act on us the way the Nairobi Indians or "Native driver" act on the oxen? Robert Langbaum says the animal fables in Part IV "are unequaled in any modern writer I know of."

"OF THE TWO RACES"

Note that Dinesen uses a sobering bombshell as her opening sentence. As a feminist, Dinesen was ahead of her time, drawing a parallel between the white race's suppression of the black race and men's suppression of women. Moral: An important ingredient of racial or sexual "supremacy" is self-delusion; the supremacist rationalizes and justifies his oppression of others with the mistaken belief that they need him more than he needs them.

"A WAR - TIME SAFARI"

This Note is commendable for the way it catches the atmosphere of wartime, the excitement of being uprooted and sent to strange places, the sudden spate of and awe of wild rumors, the way the civilian must suddenly learn new trades. Also implicit in the account is Dinesen's undisguised respect for an enemy general and her taking over, in World War I, the full field duties of a man. The general's naughty inscription on his gift photograph can be translated like this:

> Paradise on Earth Is on the back of a horse. And the goodness of body On the bosom of a woman.

"THE SWAHELI NUMERAL SYSTEM"

Moral: A prudish attitude toward reality can produce serious gaps in knowledge. (In the nineteenth century, students had to study human anatomy from charts that left a big hole in the lower torso.) Moral: The human mind will attempt to close all gaps in knowledge, using imagination where it lacks facts.

"I WILL NOT LET THEE GO EXCEPT BLESS ME"

The title is taken from the scene in Genesis in which the patriarch Jacob is wrestling with an angel who wants to end the strife, but Jacob won't release the divine wrestler unless he blesses Jacob first. Langbaum, in his insightful study of Dinesen, says that the moral of this "Notebook" segment is "that each thing that happens to us, good or bad, is a blessing... . [but] it is only by letting go that we turn it into a blessing." The Latin phrase "No coitus interruptus" that Dinesen's farmer utters - when he's afraid the rain will stop - refers to sexual intercourse interrupted to prevent impregnation.

Dinesen's **allusion** to music - "An arietta you can take da capo, but not a whole ... symphony" -means you might be inclined to repeat a short song from the very beginning but not an hour - long four -movement orchestral work. Dinesen's moral here is that we should not want - as the old lady at the party wanted - to live our lives over again unless they went badly. Her last line promises to accept life's end as she has accepted the rest of it - as a blessing.

"THE ECLIPSE OF THE MOON"

This slight piece has little to commend it except for two ideas better illustrated elsewhere in the book: The tragic failure of communication between cultures, and the reliance of the entire area, even of technical personnel, on the Baroness for guidance.

"NATIVES AND VERSE"

This is a puzzling Note. Since we have tapes of Africans singing and chanting **stanzas** of songs, it's strange to hear Dinesen say "they know nothing of verse." But later we realize she is using the word "verse" and even the word "poetry" to mean only rhymed verse. Strange again, since in "Wings" she says "I made a poem" and it turns out to be an unrhymed, free - verse poem. Then she says the Natives refused to improvise rhymes, although what they do speak is a rhyme:

Speak again. Speak like rain.

Is there some covert **irony** here?

Note in passing that the word Malaya, used without exact translation in "Big Dances," is here translated as "whores."

"OF THE MILLENIUM"

Jesus preached the coming of the Kingdom of God, often in parables. It was understood that he would return to reign on earth for 1000 years (in Latin, Millennium). And so Dinesen writes her version of what the Millennium would turn out to be. As this is a parable, there can be many interpretations. Here's one: When "joy was universal" and everything was perfect, Jesus found it boring and felt nostalgic for the old days of struggle, when even He had to suffer to triumph. He wanted to visit the Hill of Calvary (Golgotha), where He had been crucified. This would fit in with Dinesen's philosophy that we should live dangerously (see "Wings") and that even bad things are a blessing (see "I Will Not Let Thee Go …" and our note on it above) that we should embrace.

"KITOSCH'S STORY"

This famous story is related thematically to "The Wild Came …," "I Will not Let Thee Go" "Of the Two Races," and "Wamai." A rereading of those sections to relate them to the "Kitosch Story" is helpful in understanding both "Kitosch" and the overall network of ideas in *Out of Africa*.

The twofold thrust of the story is (1) Dinesen's demonstration that white people trying the case failed to understand the African psyche and (2) Dinesen's own interpretation of Kitosch's behavior.

Just as Nature retaliated against the manager by depriving him of his buffalo - ox in "The Wild ...," so here the African Native dies by his own free will and deprives the settler both of his servant and of his ability to kill the servant.

According to Dinesen, the African, operating from his grave, saved the settler from a charge of murder, a further display of the African's power over his tormentor. But using Dinesen's own description of Kitosch's state of mind, the reader can independently deduce that Kitosch, by willing himself to death, still punished his torturer by making him guilty at least of "grievous hurt."

Dinesen's insightful characterization of Kitosch is equaled by her characterization of the white man as a furious sadist who just "could not let Kitosch go" but had to return to resume the punishment. Kitosch, however, could let go.

American readers today who are astonished that the settler got only two years in jail have to be reminded that at the time of "Kitosch's Story" (in the 1930s), any American Southerner who so beat a black man probably would never have been brought to trial at all.

"SOME AFRICAN BIRDS"

These beautiful observations about birdlife in Kenya deserve at least two literary comments, one about Dinesen's analogical language, the other about her themes. (1) Note that in the sentence about Crested Cranes beginning with the phrase "The whole ballet," that **metaphor** is followed by two "like" **similes** which make both the angels and the birds resemble a ballet chorus. (2) Note that Dinesen's **theme** of sympathy for the flamingoes tortured at sea offsets her earlier enthusiasm for killing African wildlife ("Wings").

"PANIA"

There are three things at least to observe in the literary quality of this anecdote: (1) Dinesen's arresting opening sentence. (2) Her likening of dog laughter to Native laughter. (3) Her gradually moving from her convincing description of Pania's ability to laugh to her fantasy that he also talks, her way of stating that in their intimate relationship she can translate his action into human language. (See Idea 67 in our chapter 5, part A).

"ESA'S DEATH"

Langbaum makes two valuable observations about this Note: (1) that Esa's "patient, enduring life of service" parallels that of the oxen ("The Oxen"); (2) that it shows the artful arrangement of Part IV that the two stories about Esa are widely separated to suggest the passage of time between them. We should add that Esa's treatment of his second wife as "property" reinforces Dinesen's feminist **themes** (e.g., "The Somali Women"), and the fact that Mohammedan law makes it easy for Fatoma to escape punishment as a murderer reinforces Dinesen's **theme** of "poetic justice" ("The Wild ...").

"OF NATIVES AND HISTORY"

This meditation on the time it would take Natives to "catch up" with European civilization ought to be analyzed along the lines of questions like these: (1) Do Third World people have to take the same path to reach the same stage of Western development? For example, after the Chinese Revolution, Western peoples consoled themselves that since illiteracy was widespread in China, it would take them generations to "catch up." But the Chinese bypassed literacy by teaching orally and accepting tapes dictated and recorded by students in lieu of written papers and doctoral theses. And so in many areas of science China has caught up. (2) Do Third World people necessarily have to emulate Western culture in order to "progress"? Might they not open up new stages of civilization hitherto unknown to the Western mind (such as those suggested in Jamake Highwater's *The Primal Mind* or John Collier's *The Long Hope*)? (3) Do Dinesen's remarks about belief "in evolution and not in any sudden creative act" still hold true in biology and anthropology today?

"THE EARTHQUAKE"

This two-page Note shows again the fecundity of Dinesen's mind: Any event she experiences produces an outpouring of exciting insights and free associations. And again, the outpouring is a combination of humor and seriousness, as when she notes that the intervals between shocks "gave people time to form their ideas of the happening." And she cannot resist the mischievous impulse to mock the middle-class which, in its love of security and solidity, must be shocked to hear that she enjoyed the shocks of an earthquake. As usual, her free associations include **allusions** to great people. The full name and dates of the man who "found the laws of the movement of the planets" are Johannes Kepler (1571–1630), a German astronomer. Eppur si muove is the remark attributed to the Italian astronomer Galileo Galilei (1564–1642) after he was forced by the Inquisition to swear that the earth stands still: Nevertheless, it does move.

"GEORGE"

This anecdote serves three literary purposes. (1) It adds the sea-voyage dimension to the African-farm adventure. (2) Dinesen's pretense she is Hottentot adds to our experience of her mischievous wit. (3) Her characterization of the boy adds to the Romantic ideology of the book: Because he is still a "naive" child, he is uncorrupted by national/racial prejudices.

"KEJIKO"

This short Note sounds again another of Dinesen's themes: Our perception depends on our point of view.

"THE GIRAFFES GO TO HAMBURG"

Through contrast and colorful details of two different environments, Dinesen strengthens a few of her earlier themes. The European white man not only subjugates the giraffes the way he enslaves the African people, he also imagines he is good to the giraffes as he is (he thinks) a godsend to the Natives. The Shah's daughter's insistence on her rights (in the 1840s) reminds us how long the feminist struggle has been in progress. By giving us first a rich picture of the African landscape, Dinesen makes the scene of the giraffes' captivity and future home all the more pathetic.

"IN THE MENAGERIE"

Both the characterization and the ideas discussed deserve scrutiny. Dinesen makes both characters unattractive, at least at the beginning (as she did with Emmanuelson in "A Fugitive Rests ..."): the showman because of his dirty environment, sick appearance, and shady past (did he get the syphilitic nose from his scandalous behavior?); the Count because he works with other people's ideas instead of developing his own. In saying wild animals don't exist until a human mind perceives them, that giraffes can't see a square because they have no concept of a square, the Count is dabbling in the philosophy of Immanuel Kant. In answering that anything can exist if God sees it, the showman is dabbling in the philosophy of George Berkeley. The Count takes the traditional Judeo-Christian view that revulsion from serpents is instinctive, but the showman's position that God created good and evil is closer to Dinesen's (and the Africans') view.

Is the showman, like Emmanuelson, bisexual? His uncritical espousing of the legend of the hyena's bisexuality raises the question. Again like Emmanuelson, the showman has had to struggle to gain our respect, as he begins to do only at the end. The entire four - page work impresses us as incomplete, unresolved.

"FELLOW - TRAVELLERS"

The three - way conversation reveals attitudes toward Natives (in Mexico and the African Congo) that are shocking to Dinesen. Her mistake in French was this: She incorrectly used the French word travaille to mean traveled, thus saying not Have you travelled much? but Have you worked much? This is why the Belgian discourses endlessly - and defensively? - about his "labors." Ironically, his work seems to be to get the Congolese to work for him (instead of for themselves): Il faut enseigner aux negres a etre honnetes et a travailler (It is necessary to teach the blacks to be honest and to work). Getting them to labor on his behalf is part of his grande mission dans le Congo (grand mission in the Congo). As we know from earlier sections, Dinesen is not in sympathy with "missionaries" from Europe. The Belgians were notorious exploiters of the Africans and their natural resources.

"THE NATURALIST AND THE MONKEYS"

The professor's aims and attitudes give us one more instance of the European's contempt for Africa. This is probably why Dinesen thinks God would not recognize "the existence of Professor Landgreen." Since she probably substituted a fictitious name for the original person, has she chosen "Landgreen" for its irony?

"KAROMENYA"

This touching narrative demonstrates once again Dinesen's talents as a practical psychologist. She understood intuitively that the deaf-and-dumb boy's picking fights and other displays of strength were -like his stealing simply to give the loot to others - efforts to make contact with his fellow human beings.

"POORAN SINGH"

This piece is remarkable because it shows us that stage of civilization that Dinesen prefers. Her blacksmith shop is a throwback to the pre-Industrial Age, with its master training his apprentices, each of their products completely custom-made and hand - made, their workplace an exciting social center as well. The plough, the sword and cannon, the wheel - all are there, Dinesen says, and that's "civilization in a nut."

To explain the psychological appeal for visitors, Dinesen uses two appropriate metaphors: (1) Iron in the forge sets their imagination traveling on long tracks; (2) The hammer sings whatever song the visitor wants to hear.

Pooran Singh she describes in terms of paradox and contrast. In manner he is demonic at work, but gentle in his off - duty hours. Dressed, he is portly and slow; stripped to the waist at the forge, he is slight and swift. His furious work transforms him. By contrast his son works not with a hammer, but with a fountain pen.

It's clear from the author's excitement over the smithy's shop that it would be fine with her if technology had stopped right there.

"A STRANGE HAPPENING"

Dinesen establishes a magical dreamlike setting that suddenly produces a wartime nightmare and ends, as it began, in suspense. No sooner does her typical topic sentence alert us to something wondrous than she shifts suspensefully to the quality of African air which she describes with unusual words -loomings, oscillates - and with a typically opposite **simile**: it "vibrates like the string of a violin." Then when the mysterious herd appears in the distance, she creates more suspense by describing her own dog's anxiety and the difficulty of identifying animals in the midday sun. The **climax** comes in the Natives' reactions:

Those are carrion - eaters and this is wartime. We are left with an unarticulated question: Where is there a battlefield of dead large enough to attract such a long horde of wild dogs?

"THE PARROT"

This Note is appropriate as the final section for Part IV because of its symbolism and its themes. The parrot symbolizes the problems of communication and raises the question why the English lover would have taught the bird an ancient Greek poem. Is it that he knew the China - woman would have to ask many people what it meant, thus prolonging his relationship with her? And did he want too to reach in this manner another person familiar with Sappho, great writer of love lyrics seven centuries before the common era? The message from Sappho, finally translated for the old Chinese woman, has its unspoken parallel for Dinesen: It was Denys who taught her Greek poetry, and she too is now alone.

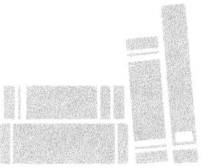

OUT OF AFRICA

TEXTUAL ANALYSIS

PART V: FAREWELL TO THE FARM

The Fall from the climactic height of Part III - postponed by the miscellaneous events and meditations of Part IV - comes inevitably in Part V with the sense of Fate that Dinesen has manifest all along. The very key words of the titles of Part V point the way downhill: "Farewell …," "Hard Times," "Death …," "The Grave …," "… Sell Out," "Farewell."

HARD TIMES

Structure

This chapter - in which Dinesen explores both the objective and subjective aspects of her loss of the farm - she divides into three parts. The first establishes most of the reasons the farm failed; it is remarkable for the way the tone of the writing varies with each failure alternating with new hope. The second narrates, at length, in a great display of colorful details and **imagery**, one of the main reasons for failure: the repeated assaults of the grasshoppers, "the days of the locusts." The third is a candid and extraordinary recollection of her psychological maneuvers to avoid facing the truth.

Metaphor, symbolism, expressionism

All the metaphoric language is bitter. After Dinesen is forced to sell her herd of cows, the "cattledip ... stood like a sunk and overturned ruin of a castle in the air." The storks and cranes eat the grasshoppers like "pompous profiteers." After Dinesen hears the bad news from Farah, her bare, bleak, and stifling hotel room becomes a symbol of her whole world. Near the end she explores her feelings with expressionistic techniques: she projects her emotions on to the landscape. She imagines, for example, that the hills know she will be leaving, and that they disengage from her and stand back so that she can see them better in her memories.

Sensuous details

Once again the narrator selects the most dramatic and sensuous details to imprint a scene on our memories. What better way to make us see the impact of millions of grasshoppers on the farm than to say that the scenery "began to quiver" and when they sat in a tree, it broke and that the wagon - wheel grooves in the road were marked out with dead insects?

Dramatic moments

Each of the first two sections is expository until the narrator reaches the crisis. Then, in a shift of mode, she uses dialogue.

The narrator has built suspense as, for hours, Dinesen hesitates to ask Farah for -and he hesitates to volunteer - information about the size of the crop. Then her fate is sealed in two gestures and three words: "he half closed his eyes and laid back his head ... 'Forty tons, Memsahib.'" And after she has told an Indian that she's begun to doubt that the grasshoppers will ever really come, he says, "Turn around kindly, Madam." And there she sees a shadow on the sky.

Psychological maneuvers

Dinesen's confessions of her mental weakness at this period are so authentic and powerful, they remind us of the greatest works in this genre, e.g., of Meyer Levin's *Obsession*. Note that her hope that she will not, after all, lose the farm (even after it's been sold) is based on the sensible observation that the world is not regular or predictable. She even resorts in her misery to making superstitious deals with Fate, to accept defeat in all other matters if she can be spared on this one central matter. Note that the woman who in earlier chapters always worried about how much time was left now has learned a lesson in living for the moment.

Breakdown in noblesse oblige

The most astonishing confession is one that Dinesen seems unaware she's made. The feudal lady of the manor once believed in noblesse oblige, i.e., that high rank imposes on the rank - holder responsibilities for the lower ranks. And now Dinesen is astonished that her Natives are waiting for her to help them as the farm faces closure, and "did not ... attempt to arrange their future for themselves." But feudalism teaches the "lower ranks" that, in return for their labor and their loyalty, they will be protected, their future will be taken care of. She has no right, at the end, to expect them to act any other way than the way they were taught to act. She seems unaware that it is she, objectively speaking, who has broken the bargain.

Real life vs. semi - autobiography

In real life, Dinesen's enterprise suffered from the fact that all her capital had been wasted by her husband's mismanagement of the farm. In *Out of Africa*, the character Dinesen simply says, "it had all been spent ... before I took over ..."

Irony

Perhaps the bitterest realization in this bitter chapter is Dinesen's feeling that the Natives were better prepared for this **catastrophe** because of their "superior inside knowledge of God and the Devil." This is a curt reference back to her earlier explanation of Native views of God: that He and the Devil are One. Note that at the end she counts the hours until she will see the Natives again.

THE DEATH OF KINANJUI

Opening phrase

Note that the chapter begins with a transitional phrase, "In that same year," which makes it clear that all her calamities have fallen on her almost at once.

Betrayal

Dinesen sees treachery and violation as the main **themes** of Kinanjui's dying and death. She seems to suspect that the king's daughter nursed him only half - heartedly, or maybe even destructively, suggesting some kind of intrigue. The existence of three groups, each meaning to put their candidate on Kinanjui's throne, adds to the nasty, ominous atmosphere. Dinesen's decision not to let the king die that night in her house seems even to her to be a betrayal of their good relationship; but to the reader perhaps the most treacherous part is the way she refuses to give him reasons. This convinces us that she is intent on making every black situation blacker. And so, when she hears the cock crow, she lets us infer the symbolism: Jesus had predicted that Peter would be disloyal to Jesus three times before the cock had crowed. She chooses to end the chapter with Farah's grave disillusionment over her abandonment of Kinanjui.

Violation by the clergy

As Dinesen sees it, the Church has also violated the Natives' rights. We would expect by now that she would be sympathetic to the Native's own "heathen" tradition of returning the dead quickly to Nature, and that she would be appalled by the Church's insistence on Christian rites of burial. Her **diction** expresses her abhorrence of the Church's exploitation of the death as an opportunity for the Church to dominate the situation: she sees the plain as "black" with clergyman, the assemblage settling "like flies" at the grave, the Christians braying - bray is a word used to describe the harsh cries of the jackass, the donkey.

Symbolism

In addition to encouraging the reader to hear the cock's crowing as symbolic of her betrayal, Dinesen seems to see other symbols throughout the process of dying and burying. Kinanjui's once flashy car has rusted, a sure symbol of dying an decay. The Church provides a coffin too small for this big man, seeming to symbolize a diminution, a belittling of his stature.

Fisher King symbolism

Was Dinesen aware of the anthropological classic *The Golden Bough*, by Sir James Frazer? In it she would have seen, as the student of contemporary literature can't miss seeing, an archetype for Kinanjui's death. Frazer's researches revealed to him a pattern of death and renewal quite universal in world myths. The pattern is typified by the myth of the Fisher King who dies of a wound in the thigh. Dinesen's intensely realistic description of Kinanjui's wound establishes an extraordinary parallel to the Frazer myth.

THE GRAVE IN THE HILLS

Tone

By writing about Denys Finch - Hatton's death and burial in a subdued, almost objective way by muting and restraining her expression of her own grief, Dinesen makes it sound as if she is still in a state of disbelief and shock, and she makes us experience and express the grief on her behalf. Denys' end brings out none of the bitterness she revealed over Kinanjui's death and burial, except for one flash of sarcasm in the paragraph about the Bishop of Nairobi and "another clergyman."

Self - characterization

Dinesen's achieving an authentic voice is nowhere more evident than in her honest confessions of her mental state. What she now calls a "compulsive idea," namely that she was surrounded by distrust and suspicion, sounds at first like paranoia. Actually, as she recalls its origins in World War I, when she was wrongfully suspected of being a German agent, we can see that it is closer to social paranoia, that is, paranoia engendered by objective, external conditions. Dinesen also seems to ignore other reasons why the middle - class people in the colony would be distrustful of her: She is friendly to the Natives, not treating them as inferiors as she is supposed to, according to bourgeois bias; she is a woman who refuses to accept a woman's place in the bourgeois world; she does not go to church and seems to be skeptical of organized religion. No wonder she sniffs detachment and rejection all about her.

The frank way in which she talks of her "derangement," her "beginning to go mad," her need to "get back my balance of mind," is in itself indication of strong character, akin to what we admire most in self - analytic texts like Meyer Levin's *Obsession* and Jean - Jacques Rousseau's *Confessions*.

Characterization: Finch - Hatton

Dinesen accomplishes in the same chapter a characterization of Denys' state of mind as well. He too has good reasons to be melancholy, even before he seems to have premonitions of his own death. His experience in searching for a new abode must have been very depressing: a man who loves the African landscape seeing at first - hand what developers are doing to a beautiful countryside. Also, he is in an unacknowledged dilemma: He is going to lose

Dinesen but he can't give up Africa and his own freedom to follow her where she must go. Her farm has been a center of culture and cultured society such as he might not find again in Africa. Another paradox in his life: like Dinesen, he dislikes, distrusts much of modern technology. There has been trouble with his airplane which, on the one hand, is his "magic carpet" to freedom and mobility, but is, on the other hand, a machine that can fail. Why did Airway's "boy" refuse to fly with Denys even after he had delivered a new part to Denys? Notice that Denys returns quickly just minutes after takeoff - had he discovered that the part was faulty and he was in a race against death?

Notice too that when he drove back, in his car, to get a book of poems, he read Dinesen a poem about geese flying away. It certainly did seem as if he had premonitions of a permanent separation between them. But he also had good reason to hate the future of Africa that he saw shaping up.

Allusions

The poem about the need for a "merry" rather than a "mournful ditty," which Dinesen says Denys "quoted ... to me" is really a traditional song. Either Dinesen misremembered (as she did with the lines from Byron's Waltz), or Denys himself adapted the song, for the actual words are:

Let me set my mournful ditty To a merry measure. Thou wilt never come for pity, Thou wilt come for pleasure.

Dinesen again resorts to *Arabian Nights* (the source of her **allusion** to Sinbad the Sailor) to describe the Swaheli fisherman. And at the very end of the chapter she strikes an echo of a famous line from an Ode by the Latin poet Horace:

Dulce et decorum est pro patria mori Sweet and decorous is it to die for one's country

Dinesen's **allusion** - "It was fit and decorous that the lions should come to Denys' grave and make him an African monument" - leads her to a remarkably sweet and fitting comparison: Lord Nelson's lions, in Trafalgar Square, are "made only out of stone."

Thomas' "V.C."

Notice that the distrust of Dinesen's sympathies during World War I dissipated only after her brother won a "V.C." for service with the British army in France. The Victoria Cross is Britain's highest military award. The East African Standard could run the headline:

An East - African V.C. because Thomas Dinesen had lived on his sister's farm long enough to be known as an "East African." She omitted an account of his stay with her as part of the process of selecting - and - rejecting that goes into the making of a work of art.

Symbolism and metaphor

In the somber context of Dinesen's account, the lions stand at the end as a natural symbol of Denys' belonging to Nature. The mist too becomes a symbol of Dinesen's own state when she cries out "I cannot see where we are." She also personifies the hills again, saying that "they themselves took charge of the ceremony ... ." An excellent **metaphor** that she uses not only sums up Finch - Hatton's life but also reminds us of Dinesen's fatalism: "The bowstring was released ... at Eton, the arrow described its orbit, and hit the obelisk in the Ngong Hills."

Of course, once the bowstring had snapped, the course of the arrow had already been determined.

FARAH AND I SELL OUT

Structure

Dinesen divides her penultimate chapter into five parts, the first distinguished especially by her remarks on Farah and her adventures with books; the second adding to the characterization of Pooran Singh and Denys Finch-Hatton; the third devoted to her famous call for a sign and the resultant parable of the chameleon and the cock; the fourth adding to the characterization of Ingrid Lindstrom and leading to a generalization about differences in male and female psychology; and the last section devoted to the political problem of the squatters on her farm.

Characterization: Farah

Without recognizing it as such, or attempting to explain it, Dinesen uncovers a paradox in Farah's behavior. As they sell off her possessions and the house becomes bare, it approaches a state, she says, "more fit to live in... ." We can understand that for her, living in it now is more like camping with its simple improvisations. And true, as she says, the house is now Das Ding an sich, German for "the thing itself, in its own right." Then Farah agrees it's more fit to live in because, she says, "all Somali" are somewhat ascetic.

However, as Dinesen's life becomes plainer and more threadbare, Farah suddenly starts to wear his most expensive and elaborate finery, not just on special days but every day.

Why? Was he trying to compensate for her loss of status? In any event, like many of Dinesen's generalizations, this one about Somali asceticism doesn't stay valid for long.

Characterization: Pooran Singh

The relationship between feudal lord and serf is well illustrated in this last glimpse of Singh. Dinesen describes him as a child "outside his workshop," and it's clear she fosters the motherchild class distinction. He wants, as a farewell present, a ring, and by selling some furniture, she manages a "heavy gold" one with a red stone which "shone like a little star while it went up and down waving goodbye." But was this artificer really such a boy with a new toy?

Characterization: Finch - Hatton

The way Denys acts over the "Abyssinian ring of soft gold" sounds the first sour note in the relationship between him and the narrator or, more likely, the first sour note she has allowed to be recorded. Here he seems capable of sulky meanness, maybe even with a trace of racist resentment of her "colored people." It makes us realize that her portrait of him up to this point has been idealized, a throwback to the "whitewash" biographies of the nineteenth century.

Characterization: Ingrid Lindstrom

Dinesen's tribute to Ingrid makes it clear how much Dinesen needed the sympathy of another "woman farmer." Some of the best writing of the book is produced by this memory: "we closed our minds round the disaster of the house.... We walked together ... as if Ingrid were, on my behalf, collecting material for a book of complaints to be laid before destiny." Noting that Ingrid could honestly act as if she was glad that the disaster had not hit her, Dinesen ventures the generalization that "Men ... cannot [so] easily or harmoniously envy or triumph over one another." The validity of this hypothesis might well be tested in the Personality Lab of any psychology department. How? Authors, especially so long ago as 1935, rush in where psychologists fear to tread.

The chameleon and the cock

This is one of the most poignant and bitter passages in Part V. Dinesen evokes our sympathy with her feeling that there must be some "central principle" behind all of her reverses. Some readers might challenge her contention that calling for "a sign" is the way to discover "the coherence of things." Dinesen does not consider the possibility that she would unconsciously pick, out of all of the morning phenomena, that event that would most confirm what she already believed. It would then be a sign from her own Unconscious, not from "the powers to which I had cried." Even so, her procedure has value as a "projective test," making the unconscious conscious. Certainly the "sign" she gets is just one more confirmation of her suspicion that the Natives are right, God and the Devil are One. The chameleon making a hopeless gesture of defiance with its tongue, the cock plucking out the tongue, Dinesen having to kill the chameleon to save it from "a slow, painful death," this is the universe "in a miniature format."

Allusion to Job

Dinesen must feel that in calling for a sign, she had got the same answer Job had got in the Old Testament, namely that God had not intended to create a cozy world, just a sublime one. But Dinesen is not so resigned as Job was. She takes a line from the Book of Job - in which God praises the warhorse who "saith among the trumpets, Ha, ha!" - and she adapts it to her situation: Great powers had laughed to me, ... they had said among the trumpets, among the cocks and Chameleons, Ha, ha!

Other literary allusions

Dinesen's account of how literary characters follow you around through your day is one of her most fanciful passages. Crome Yellow is a countryhouse **satire**, the first novel by Aldous Huxley whose masterwork was *Brave New World*. Walter Scott was a Romantic poet and novelist, whose Ivanhoe is well - known to American students. "Odysseus and his men" would be that diminishing band of Ithacans of whom only Odysseus reaches home in Homer's **epic**, *The Odyssey*. Peter Schlemihl is the poor young man who surrenders his shadow to the Devil in exchange for a magic purse in Adelbert von Chamisso's *The Strange Story of Peter Schlemihl*. Jean Racine was a leading seventeenth - century tragic dramatist. As we can tell from all our paragraphs on Dinesen's allusions, she was a voluminous reader.

Segregation of the squatters

The final section is valuable as a social document and as further characterization of the narrator. She has a good sympathetic understanding of "the primal mind" and its attachment to place and to tribe. She gives us good evidence of how the tribal mentality suffers because the European colonists can't understand people with such attachments. And of course, when we come to her statement that "it was really a problem to find ... an unoccupied stretch of land big enough to take in the full number of the people and their cattle," we wonder how she can be so restrained. It is a problem, after all, only because the white settlers have pushed the Natives into "Reserves" and kept the best lands for themselves. She tells us later that she did bear in mind that not long before, "the Natives ... had held their land undisputed, and had never heard of the white men and their laws." We are disappointed, though, that she lets the white masters off so easy.

FAREWELL

Dinesen's final chapter is noteworthy for:

- her descriptions of her mental states in these last days;

- her account of the status of old people in Africa, in which she uses a pastiche of Bible lines for a highly unusual effect;

- her closing paragraph with its symbolic tieback to the very opening passage of the book.

Status of African elders

Dinesen's descriptions of the old men preparing for the Ngoma to honor her, and of the old women who call her "Jerie," make it clear that in Africa the elderly are respected and the dread of aging is greatly lessened as a result. Note that nobody has to try to look younger, for tribal custom apportions honors and roles to people of all ages.

Biblical pastiche

As part of her paean of praise for "the old Kikuyu women," Dinesen adapts five scattered verses from the Book of Job to describe them. She makes a strong point for equality of the sexes when she adapts each line about a male animal to make them all female. Thus Job 39:29, about the male eagle, becomes "she seeketh, ... her eyes... ." Job 41:15-16, about the male Leviathan, becomes "Her heart... ." Job 39:22, about the male warhorse, becomes "She mocketh at fear... ." Job 39:18, about the female ostrich, remains "... she lifteth ... , she scorns... ." Job 40:27, again about the male Leviathan, becomes "Will she speak soft words... ."

Here Dinesen has used the technique of pastiche as artfully, for her purpose, as T.S. Eliot uses it for his in *The Waste Land*. The old Kikuyu women are described in the very terms God used to describe some of his strongest and most dramatic creatures.

Mental states

As we have already seen in the earlier chapters of Part V, Dinesen succeeds in recapturing many extreme psychological states that her reverses had plunged her into. In this chapter she recreates three more such events. As she watches the old men "in a slow prelusive march," she has the feeling that it is not she who is leaving Africa, but Africa that is leaving her. This feeling seems to be based on a mental blending of time and space: the Africans are leaving her by becoming older.

Dinesen builds up suspense before describing her next mental state. After several hundred words about the old dancers as "a rare, sublime sight," she describes the arrival of a messenger from the authorities forbidding the dance. Nothing could be more symbolic of the white settlers' interference in the freedom of the Africans than this banning of the Ngoma in honor of Dinesen. Her five paragraphs beginning "During all my life in Africa ..." is a masterful description of her outrage amidst the resignation of the old men.

The literary highpoint of the chapter comes in her magnificently compact description of the numbing sensation of departure from a major place in one's existence: "Those who have been through such events can ... say they have been through death, - a passage outside the range of imagination, but within the range of experience."

Symbolic close

For her closing moment, Dinesen describes the Ngong Hills as she glimpses them on her last train ride away from the farm. We realize at once that she is closing the circle, referring us back to the opening pages of her first chapter, "The Ngong Farm." The mountain is still noble. But what she once called the four noble peaks now look trifling, different. And she concludes with one more fine **metaphor** in what has been a rich series of figures of speech: "The outline of the mountain was slowly smoothed and leveled out by the hand of distance."

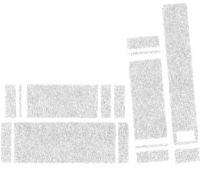

OUT OF AFRICA

CHARACTER ANALYSES

In recreating a person who is part of her life in Africa, Dinesen is likely to use two techniques of characterization: authorial exposition and dramatization.

Her exposition will include overviews of a person's career and reputation; her own impressions of the person's physique, manner, and character; generalized narration of that person's typical activities; all these elements are described with generous, life - instilling use of metaphor, allusion, significant details, and comparisons.

Dinesen is dramatizing when she actually sets a scene and has her character talking and otherwise interacting with other characters. The distinction is that in exposition we hear only the author's voice; in dramatization we're more likely to hear the character's voice.

Dinesen, like all writers of artistic nonfiction, moves freely from exposition to scene. Her description of a person's life often leads up to a situation with dialogue, and such a dramatized situation may then lead her to some opinion, character analysis, or philosophizing.

Note that as we study the following techniques Dinesen uses to characterize nineteen individuals, we naturally find we have our own opinions of some of the characters or of her characterization -final evidence that the author has brought them alive for us.

BELKNAP, DINESEN'S MILL MANAGER

Even though he figures in an important scene on the night of the shooting accident, Dinesen gives him no chance to speak in his own voice. Instead she summarizes his report to her and gives us an intense analysis of his psychological state, even as he's standing there. She makes him sound like some type of manic - depressive. Her conclusion is based on typing him as one of the "energetic young white men" who have spent their early life in towns and become mentally unbalanced in rural Africa. Apparently she feels that his present life - as "inspired mechanic" and "keen poultry farmer" - is not "heroic" enough for him. He made "very little" of his report, she concludes, "for it held no part in it for him to play, and fate had let him down once more."

When Dinesen keeps us at arm's length from a character this way, we naturally do some thinking on our own. Is that what she intends when she is suggestive like this? We wonder, isn't there a chance that his stuttering on this night is due to his feeling guilty for having left a loaded gun within reach of a child? And if he is of a "heroic" bent, might not be resent - in those dark ages of machismo - working for a woman?

BULPETT, CHARLES, ENGLISH GENTLEMAN LIVING IN NAIROBI

Dinesen characterizes him in two ways: (1) Authorial Description. In her own expository voice, she tells us of the highlights of his career and comments on them. Since he has traveled everywhere and tasted every dish, she trusts his judgment of Kamante's cooking. He was one of the first to climb the Matterhorn. He has swum the Hellespont - the famous mile - wide strait of the Dardanelles - in emulation of Lord Byron (who did it to emulate the classical hero Leander). Obviously he is important to Dinesen because he is aristocratic, heroic, and worldly. (2) Dramatization. Dinesen also recreates a dinner scene at which she and Bulpett discuss his legendary affair with La Belle Otero, and a picnic scene at which he, Denys, and Dinesen discuss the desirability of having "real wings." In these scenes she portrays him as a man who thinks before he answers so that his answer will have dramatic effect.

COLE, BERKELEY, PIONEER IN AFRICA, INTERMEDIARY BETWEEN THE WHITE GOVERNMENT AND THE BLACK NATIVES

Dinesen uses four effective means to characterize Cole: (1) **Metaphor**. He is as quiet and comfort - loving as a cat, and like a cat, he makes others comfortable too. (2) Allusions. Cole was an atavist, according to Dinesen, a throwback to some pre - Industrial Revolution period of history. To describe the periods in which he would have been more at home, she says he could have "walked in and out" of the court of English King Charles II (1630-1685); he would have held his own or better in witty, urbane talk with the dramatists William Congreve (1670-1729) and William Wycherley (1640-1716). Or Cole might have been groomed for public life by Charles D'Artagnan, hero of Alexandre Dumas' *Three Musketeers and Twenty Years After*.

(3) Dramatization. Dinesen further characterizes Cole in four dramatic scenes, one in which he chides her for serving him champagne in "coarse" glassware; the second in which he awards twelve Masai chiefs medals for their wartime service; a third in which he recalls a fight with his valet; and the last in which he and Dinesen have their last talk before his death. (4) Direct Authorial Comment. When Dinesen is not characterizing Cole in action and dialogue, she herself describes him and comments, for example, on his feeling guilty about leaving England and on his memories of life at sea.

DINESEN, ISAK

Narrator of the book and also the main character

That means we must distinguish among (1) the real Baroness Blixen, born Tanne Dinesen, as she is chronicled, e.g., in Judith Thurman's biography, (2) the character portrayed by Meryl Streep in the film *Out of Africa*, and (3) the character "I," the narrator of the book *Out of Africa* who signs herself "Isak Dinesen." The last person, the one who concerns us here (3), is a character specially created by the Baroness (1). The "I" of the book does not give us a complete account of the Baroness' experiences in Africa but only those selected situations that serve her artistic purpose in writing this prose pastoral. As a matter of fact, as we've noticed in our "Textual Analysis," the Baroness even engages in some fiction writing in this supposedly nonfiction work: For example, she gives herself credit for killing a lion that Finch - Hatton killed (in real life) and she offers "Part IV" as a notebook kept in Africa but in reality written later in Europe. The "I" of *Out of Africa* is, then a character based on the Baroness Blixen but as much a literary creation as any other character in the book.

Dinesen the character

"Tania," as Berkeley Cole calls the narrator near the end of "The Noble Pioneer," is a woman of great talent for action, a great appetite for life, who rises to great heights of intellectual, philosophical, and physical ecstasy only to be overwhelmed by circumstances that bring most aspects of her life to a tragic fall. In some ways, her greatest accomplishment is her ability to endure the psychological agonies of the fall but still to recall it in full force, to survive it, and to objectify and distance it enough to be able to write about it.

And in writing about her glamorous rise and fall, she characterizes herself almost incidentally, that is, in the course of recreating other persons, places, and things she knew during her seventeen years in Africa. Her moods in interacting with others, her philosophical conclusions from her experience, her sense of responsibility, her dislikes - all of which she expresses through selected details and incidents, with great metaphoric power - finally add up to a complex and often contradictory personality.

Dinesen the refugee

She is in Africa, we infer, for the same reasons that Berkeley Cole and Denys Finch - Hatton are there. She is a voluntary refugee from European civilization, with its middle-class emphasis on urban "progress," on security without adventure, its subordination of Nature and sensuousness to vocational routine, conformity, and rationality. She and her friends realize that Europe is steadily destroying the advantages and adventures of tribal life in a magnificent environment, and that what they fled from has followed them.

Dinesen the aristocrat

She is an aristocrat and a feminist. She is the European type of aristocrat as opposed to the American type. That means that she is motivated in her relations with others by a strong sense of noblesse oblige: high rank has obligations to the people at large. (In America wealth is so seldom thought of as a concomitant of social responsibility that when a rich family shows social consciousness it is thought of, by other wealthy families, as "traitors to their class.") On the other hand, an American reader can't help being impressed by the fact that Dinesen never questions her right to her rank. At the end of Part II, she gives us a copy of a legal document, a ruling made by herself and another aristocrat - a Native king - and signed Baroness Blixen.

As an aristocrat she accepts the fact that hundreds of Native families will work for her (children included) in exchange for land she leases to them (land they once owned before the white settlers took it away from them). She knows that the system in which she is a benevolent despot also tolerates cruel and repressive land barons and officials.

Dinesen's noblesse oblige

As part of her noblesse oblige she learns to run a clinic, to provide shelter for the homeless, to judge the Natives' civil-law disputes, to run a household that is also a feudal manor. She talks always of "my Natives," "my people," "my squatters."

Dinesen the feminist

She is a feminist, but an aristocratic not a democratic one; in an age when even aristocratic women had limited rights - social, legal, and domestic - she assumes every privilege accorded to men. She serves on dangerous wartime operations in which she is in effect a field commander; she, like many men of her time - e.g., Ernest Hemingway - believes in exposure to exploration, war, and wild animals as a test of character. Her hero is the aristocratic hero (Finch - Hatton, Cole, Kinanjui); her heroine is not the typical female aristocrat but a "unisex" aristocrat like herself. She is closer to Queen Elizabeth I than to Martha Washington or Dolly Madison.

Like Elizabeth, Dinesen holds court not only in the legal sense but in the cultural sense: her manor is a salon for intellectuals, cultured lovers of the arts, and administrators of estates like herself.

Her life rises to "the most transporting pleasure" in her companionship with Finch - Hatton, with whom she learns classical languages, love of poetry and music, respect for absolute freedom of the individual from any personal obligations, and from whom she gains the opportunity to explore such "transporting" experiences as hunting lions and flying, in an airplane and on a magic carpet of imaginary flights.

DINESEN'S OBSTACLES

The obstacles she faces are cumulative and overwhelming. Her land is committed to the wrong crop for the climate, she lacks the capital to convert the land to other use, coffee prices fluctuate and her crop diminishes, locusts by the billions destroy her other revenue crops, the English suspect her of pro-German sympathies, and she loses Denys as well as Cole and Kinanjui. She explores for our benefit the unbalance of mind that such **catastrophes** cause. The one great weakness of mind she and Denys share is their inability to admit that the fall is in progress: as aristocrats they seem to feel, unconsciously, that Society and Nature always take care of aristocrats. And "her" people assume that the aristocrats will always take care of them.

No friend of institutionalized religions and "missionaries," she develops, apparently in part because of the fall, a philosophy of fate, of the need to embrace fate because (as the Natives know and Europe has forgotten) God and the Devil are the two poles of a Unity.

The real Dinesen

To appreciate fully the character Dinesen that the author Dinesen has based on the real Dinesen, we have to read also her own *Letters from Africa* and *Shadows on the Grass*, her brother Thomas Dinesen's memoir, and Judith Thurman's biography,

Isak Dinesen: The Life of a Storyteller. Thurman is especially astute in indicating which elements in Dinesen's books of fiction are also based on Dinesen's real life.

EMMANUELSON, A SWEDISH ACTOR ON THE RUN

This is one of Dinesen's most dramatic characterizations. It is developed as the working out of dramatic **irony**. At the beginning, appearances are all against this man: He is oily in manner, talkative, shabby, and unprepossessing. But gradually, through his courtesy, his knowledge of wines, his candor about his weaknesses, he begins to fascinate Dinesen and she comes to sympathize with him. Perhaps what wins her over completely is his confessio fidei (his confession of faith): "... with the exception of God I believe in absolutely nothing." These aspects of his character shine through the appearances and speak of nobler realities. His triumph comes when the Masai accept him, and he finds work and sends back the money he owes Dinesen. This complete dramatic reversal elicits a moral from the author. Emmanuelson was safe with the Masai because the true aristocrat and the true proletarian understand tragedy. The implication is there too that Dinesen could understand Emmanuelson because she too has the aristocrat's sense of tragedy.

ESA, DINESEN'S COOK BEFORE KAMANTE

Through a series of short scenes set in the midst of authorial **exposition**, Dinesen characterizes this old man as a gentle, passive victim of circumstances whose one bold step ends in disaster. She allows us to infer two messages that she only implies. (1) Esa's former mistress symbolizes the way power corrupts: because her husband could draft Esa into war - service, she can force him to return as her cook. (2) Sudden financial windfall can bring out the unexpected in a man's personality; without financial security a person may never know his/her full potential. Notice how Esa himself uses two pathetic symbols in an effort to convince Dinesen of his plight. His gift on returning to her is a painting of a tree with hundreds of leaves - a way of reminding her that he wants to be a gardener, not a cook. And to let Dinesen know how hard the official's wife makes him work, he reminds Dinesen how she once declared her belief that oxen should have one day off a week.

FARAH ADEN, A SOMALI SERVANT IN CHARGE OF DINESEN'S HOUSEHOLD

He is Dinesen's constant adviser on all domestic problems and on Native affairs. A Native, for example, must apply to Farah for an interview with Dinesen. He acts as a catalyst at the Kyama. Dinesen and Farah are so attuned to each other that a glance between them will suffice, and his facial expressions tell her what he is thinking: e.g., his face darkens with shock when she refuses to take in the dying King Kinanjui, or he closes his eyes and holds his head back when telling her about a disastrously small crop. As a Somali, according to Dinesen, he is litigious and often away on tribal lawsuits. As a Mohammedan, he has a large household of women which is one of many groups Dinesen supports on her farm. When her fortunes are so bad that he worries whether her shoes will last her on her journey home to Denmark, he himself dresses in his best clothing, "like Solomon in all his glory," apparently to maintain their status in public. In the feudalistic sense, Dinesen as Master and Farah as Servant are complementary parts of a Unity.

FATOMA, ESA'S SECOND WIFE

Apparently Dinesen has had little direct contact with Fatoma, for she describes her very briefly and reports the rest of Fatoma's story second - hand. Dinesen uses one of her incredibly unkind generalizations to describe Fatoma as having the "lasciviousness of her mother's nation [Swaheli]." Even if it's true that Fatoma escapes Esa to live with the soldiers in Nairobi, (1) must all Swaheli women be so put down on that account, and (2) doesn't Fatoma have good reason to take refuge some place from the bargain made by her father and elderly husband? What other alternative would she have in a male -dominated society with no place for a woman but bed?

FINCH - HATTON, DENYS, SAFARI HUNTER, AVIATOR, DINESEN'S BEST FRIEND

First, we must distinguish among (1) the real Finch Hatton (who did not hyphenate his name) as he is found in a factual biography, e.g., Judith Thurman's *Isak Dinesen*; (2) the Denys played by Robert Redford in Sydney Pollack's film *Out of Africa*; and (3) the Denys Finch - Hatton of the book *Out of Africa*. The last person, the one who concerns us here (3), is a character especially created for this book, a sort of essential Denys but not the complete Denys.

Dinesen characterizes Denys in her **exposition** by stressing the unique details of his personality and his influence on others, and in the scenes she chooses to dramatize, by stressing his coolness, even humorousness, in dangerous situations and his readiness to quote poetry appropriate to the immediate situation. She sums up her story with a classical **metaphor** that explains her philosophy of all human life.

FINCH - HATTON: ATAVIST

Dinesen sees Finch - Hatton, like Cole, as an atavist, a throwback to an earlier English period. She suggests the Renaissance, but we can infer too that he would have been at home in any **epic** period. She sees him as a Renaissance man, able to associate with Sir Philip Sidney or Francis Drake, because he was a fine out - of - doorsman, an adventurer, a lover of the arts, a man who could hold a weapon in one hand and a book of poetry in the other, with equal ease and effectiveness.

We can add to these **allusions** and impressions the fact that he would have been comfortable too in any period in which people listened to poetry recited: Homer's day or the days of the Anglo - Saxon **epic** poets. This ability to love poetry as it is recited singles him out as a cultured man.

We can see here too a paradox in his character. While he is more a man of a past heroic age who is uncomfortable in the twentieth century (he is depressed when he inspects the kind of bungalow the developers are building near Nairobi), he still selects from modern technology what most suits his needs: he flies in an up - to - date airplane, uses an up - to - date car, and relies on heavy - caliber rifles that must be the last word in sportsman's weaponry. Rather than put him totally in a past age, it seems better to say he straddles the past and the present.

FINCH - HATTON: MAN OF CANDOR

The tragic part of Dinesen's relationship with him is that he is a man of temperament who wants to be with her only when he wants to, and not as a regular obligation. He is, in other words, a man of candor and spontaneity, who lives close to his own feelings. But as a result, when he does want to be at her farm, it is an intense and passionate want that she knows is deeply sincere. Note such details as his playing the gramophone when he arrives so that when she comes in from out - of - doors she will know he is there. Dinesen's ingenious way of describing the effect of his arrival is to say that the house spoke: that is, when he is there, all reality comes into greater focus, his presence organizes her life, it gives her a hierarchy of values.

FINCH - HATTON'S INFLUENCE

His influence on people is characterized by Dinesen without her ever using the phrase. Her whole life changed: she learned poetry by heart, learned Greek and Latin and read the Bible: apparently all her **allusions** in this book stem from their time together loving literature. He also awakened in her a love of classical music. Other people in the Colony had reverence for his "values outside their understanding," for he lived an "unconditional truthfulness" that few people can attain.

This unconditional honesty seems linked to his courage. In Dinesen's dramatization of their lion hunts and their daily airplane flights, she puts us in the presence of a man who is brave and self - assured. When they are close to a lion he is courteous enough to ask Dinesen "Shall I shoot her?" because it's Dinesen's land and he needs her permission. But notice that the question makes it clear he has no doubt he will kill the beast; he will not just try to hit her; once Dinesen says "Yes" he will hit the target and remove the lion as a threat. In her account of the plane rides she shows too the exquisite sensuality of Finch -Hatton. He turns off the airplane engine so they can hear the screech of an eagle flying nearby. (In open cockpit airplanes one can do such things as fly quietly and listen. What would Denys say of our jet flights in which we cannot even see anything?)

Dinesen also captures in her description of his last days another paradox of his makeup: he thought of himself as a rational man but he was often in deep inexplicable moods. This is not however so paradoxical as Dinesen thinks - the Renaissance man valued rationality in its place, and mood, intuition, and insight in their places. And apparently near the end he sensed closure, for he was in a deep melancholy. When he was racing back to the airport, was it because he had found the new part defective, or wrong? Is that why the "parts" man had refused to fly with him?

FINCH - HATTON THE ARROW

Dinesen finds the perfect **metaphor** both to honor his flying - in a plane and in his imagination -and to express her own concept of Fate. "The bowstring was released on the bridge at Eton, the arrow described its orbit, and hit the obelisk in the Ngong Hills." To Dinesen, once a life was set into motion, its course could not be changed.

HIGH PRIEST FROM INDIA

Although he appears in just one chapter, he is a memorable character. Dinesen characterizes him first by relating the detailed preparations necessary for his visit: they make it clear he is a major figure to his people. Then she lets us see his importance as he arrives with his entourage, like a flight of white birds or a company of angels. Then we feel his spiritual force; even though he and Dinesen don't speak each other's language, he casts an aura over his surroundings. He has found safety and security through acceptance of Fate. Dinesen uses two effective comparisons to describe his face: it seems to be carved in very old ivory, yet it seems to be the face of a "noble infant," perhaps of the Christ child. We must remember that to a Romantic like Dinesen, the child is the most spiritual of human beings, uncorrupted as yet by the social and material world; the child is closer to God and Truth, to intuition, and to insight than the adult is.

KABERO, BELKNAP'S KITCHEN "TOTO" (BOY SERVANT)

He is only seven on the night of the shooting accident, and since he disappears for five years, Dinesen can exploit well the mystery of his disappearance and the shock of his change of personality on his return. Dinesen's understanding of the childish nature of the Toto is one of her best pieces of character analysis: he fired Belknap's shotgun "in the greatness of youth and popularity," and, alas, acting "the part of a white man." His leaving a coin behind to pay for his new clothing is the kind of poignant detail that Dinesen picks up intuitively. His return triggers from her a steady stream of perfect metaphors: the Masai took in the Toto as a "small lamb," and now sent back a "young leopard." Adopting the Masai attitudes, Kabero stretches his chin out "as if ... presenting you his sullen arrogant face upon a tray." His insolence is such that it makes of him "an object for contemplation, such as a statue is, a figure which is to be seen, but which itself does not see." This is one of the passages in which Dinesen proves she is one of the best analogical thinkers in modern literature, especially when using **metaphor** to characterize a personality.

KAMANTE, KIKUYU TRIBESMAN, DINESEN'S COOK

He is a good example both of Dinesen's ability to bring out the best in a Native and of her talent in characterizing a complex person. Although he holds most of the world in contempt, he is eternally grateful to her for treating his diseased legs and for sending him to the Scotch Mission hospital to complete the cure. His manual dexterity first becomes manifest to her when he serves as her assistant in her clinic. She finds the perfect place for him in the kitchen, where he proves to be a genius in the culinary arts. One of the highpoints of his career is the time the Prince of Wales (later King Edward VIII and finally Duke of Windsor) praises his Cumberland sauce. Yet, Kamante himself always prefers the Kikuyu dishes of his ancestors. Proud of being a Christian convert (because that makes him like Dinesen), he holds fellow Kikuyus in contempt because they fear dead bodies, and his new religion allows him to help remove dead people. Although he is caustic about most human beings and seems isolated from them, he has a natural ability with animals; he is the human hero of the chapter in which the young antelope Lulu is the heroine.

Dinesen sums up the contradictions in his character with one of her best observations: he has mastered existence but has no high opinion of it. She lavishes some of her best **metaphors** on her physical description of him: he looks like "a dark bat with very big spreading ears." He could well be a gargoyle sitting atop the Cathedral of Notre Dame in Paris.

KINANJUI, KING OF THE KIKUYU TRIBES

Dinesen composes her portrait of this memorable figure through three means: (1) **Metaphor**. Having noticed that Kinanjui has a magnificent profile, and having realized that "the profile is the true face of a king," Dinesen notes that Kinanjui's profile is "like a head struck on a medal." His nose too is impressive, "like the trunk of an elephant." His house is a center of great vitality, "like a well spouting from the ground and running over on all sides." And Dinesen uses a metaphoric contrast; while Farah is like a sheepdog, Kinanjui is an old ram. (2) Dramatization. The King is characterized in memorable scenes. Even though she does not need him at the Kyama, Dinesen invites him because his very presence lends dignity and authority to the proceedings. It's a moment of fine dramatic spectacle when he "turns his side to the screaming crowd." Dinesen shows the human side of the King when she describes his passing out from an alcoholic drink. The scene at his deathbed is one of the dramatic highlights of the book, achieved again largely through spectacle; for example, the way he keeps his eyes on her, how "he looked like a dark wooden figure roughly cut with a knife." (3) Direct Authorial Observation. As always, it's Dinesen's own personal comments that cinch her characterization. Kinanjui, she says, has the fine manner of real greatness, originality of mind, and a daring imagination. He has "the quality of being effective."

KNUDSEN, "OLD," FORMER SEAMAN

Dinesen's depiction of the old Dane, Knudsen, is one of the best in her gallery of portraits. She uses several methods to characterize him: (1) Allusions. He is as wild and ferocious as a Berserk from Scandinavian mythology; it is harder to stop him from talking than it is to stop the Ancient Mariner; he is as tenacious as the Old Man of the Sea in the story of Sinbad the Sailor. Allusive **Simile**. He is "like a Puck grown old and blind and very malicious." (2) Dramatization. Dinesen characterizes him at length by catching him at work on his charcoal - burning and dam - construction projects and recording their discussions. (3) Authorial Insights. As he rages about his past, Dinesen has two great insights into his character. First, she sees that there are two individuals in one old body. By telling about the adventures of the young Knudsen, he tries to deny the very - much - present existence of Old Knudsen. Also, he is terrified of women and apparently in flight from them. (4) Dinesen's tone. In her two sections about Knudsen she is satirical, even mocking at times. Yet there is no doubt that behind the sarcasm about his behavior she actually admires him: he too is an outcast, a refugee from European traditions; he conceives of, and carries out, vast engineering projects in which he changes Nature to suit his purposes.

LINDSTROM, INGRID, ANOTHER WOMAN RUNNING A FARM ON HER OWN

Her visit to Dinesen's farm after Denys' death triggers a beautiful passage about the value of female companionship. Dinesen says Ingrid had the "teeth of a laughing Valkyrie," and this **allusion** makes us see her as a wise, lusty, Amazonian woman.

MARTIN, HUGH, A CIVIL SERVANT IN THE LAND OFFICE

Although she introduces him only briefly here and there, Dinesen manages to depict him as a man who undergoes a profound transformation. In midbook he finds both humanity and the universe mean and contemptible; he is one of "the Devil's disciples." But after Denys dies, Dinesen finds Martin by the grave, a changed man, suddenly aged and sick - looking, as though he had had just one ideal and now that too was dead. Throughout he is depicted in terms of a **simile**: he looks like a "fat Chinese idol." His literary background is suggested in his calling Dinesen "Candide," the name of the hero of Voltaire's novel *Candide*, who is honest, open to new experience, a naif in the best sense of the word. And Dinesen has called Martin "Doctor Pangloss," after Candide's tutor. At the end Martin's erudition helps him find, in a Greek author, an **epitaph** for Denys: "Though in death fire be mixed with my dust, yet care I not. For with me now all is well."

MOHR, GUSTAV, A FARMER NEIGHBOR

He is quickly characterized by details and a **simile**. He is big - nosed, with shining light eyes, he finishes work on his own farm to come and work on Dinesen's, and he reads Knut Hamsun, a leading novelist of Mohr's native Norway. A man with a "burning mind," he is flung on to the farm "like a stone out of a volcano." He puts himself and his car at Dinesen's service when she goes up in the Hills to find the site for Denys' grave and when she rides to the train for the last time. The price she has paid for his continual help is that she can't ever get in a word of her own once he starts talking.

POORAN SINGH, INDIAN ARTIFICER ON THE FARM

In characterizing Pooran Singh and her relationship with him, Dinesen reveals the kind of society and technology she prefers: The feudal society, with its skilled artisans loyal to a master (mistress) who treats them paternalistically (maternalistically). Pooran and his forge are one mass of energy. At work there, she says, he is a servant of the gods (like Hephaestos, we assume, artificer to Hera - Dinesen and the other Olympian gods). There he is mighty, nimble, demonic, inspired, inventive. His forge represents the stage of technology Dinesen clearly wishes were still dominant today: with its small - scale enterprises, its custom - made and hand - made products, each unique and bearing the stamp of the individual craftsman, his workplace is also a place for casual socializing (like the village well). Away from his workplace, Pooran is gentle and mild - mannered, even childish. His childishness - and how she feeds it - are obvious in his asking for a ring as a farewell gift; on getting it, he is like a boy with a new toy. We are left, after the scene in which he waves farewell from the train, wondering: did he really prefer that kind of mother -child relationship, or did she bring it out in him, or had he learned that was what she wanted?

THOMPSON, MRS. DARELL, A HORSEWOMAN

Dinesen makes her memorable with just a few distinctive details: When she learns she has only a short time to live, she turns over a new pony to Dinesen; the pony carries on the prize - winning tradition of Thompson animals but also dies soon after.

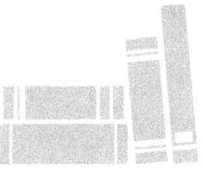

OUT OF AFRICA

QUESTIONS FOR REVIEW

Contrast the author's views on men's roles and women's roles.

Out of Africa is described as an autobiographical narrative. What major ideas does Dinesen give you about herself? Write a biography of the author from this book.

The last chapter of the book depicts a tremendous human tragedy. Define tragedy and tell what in this chapter is "tragic." Could it have been avoided?

Explain how the symbolism of the animals expresses Dinesen's ideas of strength and weakness.

Compare the idea of Utopia in *Out of Africa* with that in another work, e.g., *Paradise Lost* by John Milton. Explain the faults in each work's idea of Utopia.

Discuss the reasons Dinesen can be considered a typical or atypical woman for the time that she lived in.

Explain how personal roles in African tribes are compared or contrasted with roles of Dinesen's society.

Explain how title was important to a particular class of people, but led to their downfall.

Isak Dinesen was quite concerned about the animals on her farm. If she was alive today, would she be an environmentalist? Give specific examples from the book to support her love of animals and your answer to the question.

Select one of John Steinbeck's literary works and compare it with *Out of Africa*. Both writers are known for their figurative language. Compare the styles of each writer and list similarities and differences.

Dinesen believed that you are who you marry. Explain why she married Bror Blixen. Did she get what she wanted? Was she who she married?

Select and write about three political **themes** in this book.

Imagine that you are Isak Dinesen. Compare and contrast the white Europeans with the colored peoples in Africa. Whom does Dinesen feel most at home with? Give quotations from the book to support your comparisons.

Consider what Dinesen says about "democracy." Do you agree or disagree with her? Why?

Isak Dinesen felt she was repressed in Danish society. Why then did she become a feudal baroness in British East Africa?

Symbolism abounds in this book. Consider five symbols that the author uses. Tell what each one represents. What is the function of symbolism?

A critic has described Dinesen as a feudalist/feminist. Can a person be one and the same? Explain.

Dinesen is aware of the roles of men and women. Her perceptions of these roles are intertwined in *Out of Africa*. Mention several perceptions of men and women that she gives in her book. (You should include native Africans.)

Africa is the largest **metaphor** in the book. What does she compare Africa to?

After you read *Out of Africa*, rent the videotape for your class. Cite figurative language in the book that lends itself to film. Could Dinesen be considered a cinematographic writer?

Dinesen is a person with many pseudonyms. "Isak" is a masculine name. Given historical reasons why the author of *Letters from Africa* would choose to publish her memoirs under a pseudonym.

Write a dialogue between Kamante and the Baroness capturing the spirit of each person.

In the last chapter of the book, Isak Dinesen's society crumbles. Explain why her society crumbled.

Describe the system of feudalism as depicted on the Baroness' coffee plantation.

Imagine that you are about to interview Isak Dinesen. Write ten questions you would use for your interview. Make sure you do your research first.

Dinesen's literature abounds in contrasts and comparisons. List five things in her book that she compares. Explain their presence in her book.

What are the major **themes** of *Out of Africa*?

Dinesen had a theory that the closer you are to nature, the more real you are. Who then in her estimation was "more real" - Europeans or the Natives? Explain.

Stillness of the air and the altitude are featured in this book. What do these two things symbolize for the author?

Imagine yourself to be a European from a repressed society. You are invited to attend a native Ngoma.

a. What is a Ngoma?

b. Describe it the way Dinesen would.

c. How would you feel being there for the first time?

List several customs that the natives had that differed from the customs of the white man.

What did the Natives mean when they called something a "moth machine"?

Dinesen does a brilliant job of contrasting the judicial system of Africa and that of the white man when she relates Kitosch's story. Explain the case and contrast the judicial system of the two societies.

Describe three tribes mentioned in the book. Why does Dinesen say that the Natives are more worldly than the white man?

How did Dinesen refer to the European emigres who frequented her farm? Describe five emigres. Compare them with the Natives discussed in the previous question.

Give several reasons why Europeans emigrated to British East Africa.

What literary devices does Dinesen use in relating the story of Lulu? Be sure to explain who and what Lulu is.

What do you think was Dinesen's greatest loss as a person? Consider only the losses related in the book.

What are three reasons given in the book why the Natives and the Europeans did not understand each other?

Describe how Dinesen feels about being real and accepted for who and what one is.

Dinesen has a superb sense of humor. Relate the story of Kinanjui that she told that tells how they became such good friends.

There are many humorous anecdotes about Dinesen's relationship with Kamante. Discuss a few.

Write a book review of *Out of Africa*.

Discuss Dinesen's style of writing as romantic and pastoral. Define your terms.

If you were a filmmaker and you had to select three scenes for a movie, what scenes from the book would you select? Give reasons for your selections.

Did Dinesen believe that syphilis is a punishment? Why? What had she done in her life that she felt she deserved punishment for?

Dinesen has been described as a true aristocrat. What things did she do that qualified her on her farm to be considered an aristocrat"?

If you were comparing Dinesen to feminists in today's society, whom would she be like? Explain your choice.

Dinesen is a master at characterization. Discuss three characters in her book. What techniques does she use to characterize.

Is Dinesen a religious or spiritual person in the usual sense of the terms? Does she feel that Africa is a spiritual or religious place to be?

Contrast the Somali and Kikuyu tribes mentioned in *Out of Africa* in terms of their

  a. Rituals

  b. Customs

  c. Roles of women and men in their respective tribes.

What other setting could this story take place in? What is the importance of this setting in the story?

Dinesen uses a great deal of symbolism in describing animals of Africa. Explain what animals meant to early man during the time of the caveman as well as to the African tribesmen.

If you were a writer, what part of the book would you rewrite? Give reasons for your rewrites. Make sure that your reediting would be realistic for today's society.

The author of *Out of Africa*, published in 1937, had another book published successfully, *Seven Gothic Tales*, in 1934. Why do you think that she used the masculine pseudonym, Isak Dinesen, in publishing these books? Read "Success and the Pseudonymous Writer: Turning Over a New Self," *New York Times Magazine*, December 6, 1987.

What aspects of Dinesen's autobiographical narrative can also be considered as historical? List them and give situations from the book to explain your answers.

Critics have described this book to be pastoral prose. What does that mean? Consult a handbook of literary terms. Compare Dinesen's pastoral prose with a classic work of pastoral poetry (e.g., "October" in *The Shepherd's Calendar* by Edmund Spenser; Allen Ginsberg's *Ecologue*). For a really ambitious study, consider Dinesen's *Out of Africa* in the context of Laurence Lerner's *The Uses of Nostalgia: Studies in Pastoral Poetry*.

Compare Isak Dinesen's *Out of Africa* with Ernest Hemingway's *The Green Hills of Africa* for their different styles, themes, treatments of animals, concepts of the hero and heroism, comparisons between people and peoples.

Compare Dinesen's idea that the proud man finds happiness "in the fulfillment of his fate" ("Of Pride") with Dante's idea, at the end of *Divine Comedy*, that man finds ecstasy in blending his own free will with God's will.

"Of Pride" is a title modeled directly on the titles used by the most famous writers of personal essays - Michel de Montaigne, Francis Bacon, Ralph Waldo Emerson, among others. Consult a handbook of literary terms, or Walter James Miller's *Sourcebook for English Papers*, and try to place Dinesen's "Of Pride" in the context of the **genre** of the essay. Which type of essay is "Of Pride"? For a more ambitious study, compare Dinesen's "Of Pride," and/or "Of the Two Races," "Of the Millennium," "Of Natives and History," with one or more "Of _____" or "On _____" essays by Bacon, Montaigne, Emerson, or any of the other essayists mentioned in the handbooks or Sourcebook. What is Dinesen's precedent for being so didactic?

Draw the parallels between Dinesen's essay "The Oxen" and James Agee's classic short story, "The Mother's Tale." What do both fables say about our need to get causal perspective on our own sufferings?

Compare Dinesen's ideas in "Of the Two Races" with Eldridge Cleaver's ideas in *Soul on Ice*. The Bright Note on Cleaver will give you many leads and insights.

Read the Jacob story in the book of Genesis and report on why Dinesen alluded to it in the "Notebook" ("I Will Not Let Thee Go Except Thou Bless Me").

Analyze "Of Natives and History" in terms of the most recent studies in human evolution.

Read John Collier's *The Long Hope* and Jamake Highwater's *The Primal Mind*, both about the American Indian. What Highwater and Collier ideas could be applied to understanding Dinesen's "Natives"?

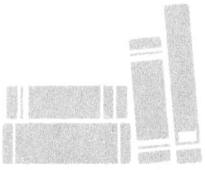

BIBLIOGRAPHY

WORKS BY ISAK DINESEN

Dinesen, Isak. *Seven Gothic Tales*. New York: Harrison Smith and Robert Haas, 1934. London: Putnam, 1934.

Dinesen, Isak. *Syv Fantastiske Fortae Llinger*. Copenhagen: Reitzels, 1935.

Dinesen, Isak. *Out of Africa*. London: Putnam, 1937; New York: Random House, 1938.

Blixen, Karen. *Den a Frikanske Farm*. Copenhagen: Gyldendal, 1937.

Dinesen, Isak. *Winter's Tales*. New York: Random House; London: Putnam, 1942.

Blixen, Karen. *Vinter Eventyr*. Copenhagen: Gyldendal, 1942.

Blixen, Karen [Pierre Andrezel]. *Genyaeldelesens Veje*. Translated into Danish by Clara Svendsen [sic]. Copenhagen: Gyldendal, 1944.

Dinesen, Isak. *Last Tales*. New York: Putnam, 1957.

Blixen, Karen. *Sidste Fortaellinger*. Copenhagen: Gyldendal, 1957.

Dinesen, Isak. *Anecdotes of Destiny*. New York: Random House; London: Michael Joseph, 1958.

Blixen, Karen. *Skoebne Anekdoter*. Copenhagen: Gyldendal, 1958.

Blixen, Karen. *Skygger Paa Groesset*. Copenhapen: Gyldendal, 1960.

Dinesen, Isak. *Shadows on the Grass*. New York: Random House; London: Michael Joseph, 1961.

Blixen, Karen [Osceola]. *Osceola*. Edited by Clara Svendsen. Copenhagen: Gyldendal, Julebog Ed., 1962.

Dinesen, Isak. *Ehrengard*. New York: Random House; London: Michael Joseph, 1963.

Blixen, Karen. *Ehrengard*. Translated into Danish by Clara Svendsen. Copenhagen: Gyldendal, 1963.

Blixen, Karen. *Essays*. Copenhagen: Gyldendal, 1965.

Blixen, Karen. *Karen Blixen's Tegninger: Med to Essay af Karen Blixen*. Edited by Frans Lasson. Copenhagen: Forening for Boglaandvaerk, 1969.

Blixen, Karen. *Efterladte Fortaellinger*. Edited by Frans Lasson. Copenhagen: Gyldendal, 1975.

Dinesen, Isak. *Carnival: Entertainments and Posthumous Tales*. Chicago: University of Chicago Press, 1977.

Blixen, Karen. *Breve Fra Africa: 1914–1931*. Edited by Frans Lasson.: Gyldendal, 1978.

Dinesen, Isak. *Daguerreotypes and Other Essays*. Translated by P. M. Mitchell and W. D. Paden. Chicago: University of Chicago Press, 1979.

Dinesen, Isak. *Letters from Africa: 1914–1931*. Edited by Frans Lasson. Translated by Anne Born. Chicago: University of Chicago Press, 1981.

WORKS ABOUT ISAK DINESEN

Arendt, Hannah. "Isak Dinesen, 1885–1962." *Men in Dark Times*. New York: Harcourt Brace Jovanovich, 1968.

Beard, Peter, Ed. *Longing for Darkness: Kamante's Tales from "Out of Africa."* New York: Harcourt Brace Jovanovich, 1975.

Bogan, Louise, "Isak Dinesen." *Selected Criticism*. New York: Noonday, 1955.

Brandes, Georg. *An Essay on Aristocratic Radicalism*. London: Macmillan, 1914.

Brandes, Georg. "Wilhelm Dinesen." *Samlede Skrifter*, Vol. 3 (1919), pp. 189–196.

Cate, Curtis. "Isak Dinesen: The Scheherazade of our Times." *Cornhill, Winter 1959–60*, pp. 120–137.

Cate, Curtis. "Isak Dinesen." *Atlantic Monthly*, December 1959, pp. 151–155.

Davidson, Basil. *A History of East and Central Africa: To the Late Nineteenth Century*. Garden City, N.Y.: Doubleday, Anchor Books, Rev. Ed., 1969.

Dinesen, Thomas. *My Sister, Isak Dinesen*. Translated by Joan Tate. London: Michael Joseph, 1975.

Hannah, Donald. *"Isak Dinesen" and Karen Blixen: The Mask and the Reality.* New York: Random House, 1971.

Henriksen, Liselotte. *Isak Dinesen: A Bibliography.* Chicago: University of Chicago Press, 1977.

Huxley, Elspeth. *White Man's Country: Lord Delamere and the Making of Kenya.* 2 Vols. New York: Praeger, 1968.

Johannesson, Eric O. *The Word of Isak Dinesen.* Seattle: University of Washington Press, 1961.

Langbaum, Robert. *The Gaiety of Vision: Isak Dinesen's Art.* New York: Random House, 1965.

Svendsen, Clara. Ed. *Isak Dinesen: A Memorial.* New York: Random House, 1965.

Svendsen, Clara. Ed. and Trans. *Karen Blixen* [Memorial Anthology]. Copenhagen: Gyldendal, 1962.

Thurman, Judith. *Isak Dinesen: The Life of a Storyteller.* New York: St. Martin's Press, 1982.

Wamberg, Bodil. *Out of Denmark.* Copenhagen: Danish Cultural Institute, 1985.

Wescott, Glenway. "Isak Dinesen." *Images of Truth* New York: Harper, 1962.

ALSO RELEVANT

Heine, Heinrich. *Selected Works.* Edited and translated by H. M. Mustard et al. New York: Random House (Vintage), 1973.

Hemingway, Ernest. *Green Hills of Africa*. New York: Scribner, 1935.

Highwater, Jamake. *The Primal Mind*. New York: NAL, 1982.

Nietzsche, F. W. *The Portable Nietzsche*. Edited and translated by Walter Kaufman. New York: Random House (Vintage), 1954.

Tales from the Thousand and One Nights. Translated by N. J. Dawood. Harmondsworth: Penguin, 1955.

www.ingramcontent.com/pod-product-compliance
Lightning Source LLC
LaVergne TN
LVHW011712060526
838200LV00051B/2880